The New Testament: A Very Short Introduction

Very Short Introductions available now:

For more information visit our web site
www.oup.co.uk/general/vsi/

Luke Timothy Johnson

THE NEW TESTAMENT

A Very Short Introduction

OXFORD
UNIVERSITY PRESS

OXFORD

UNIVERSITY PRESS

Oxford University Press, Inc., publishes works that further
Oxford University's objective of excellence
in research, scholarship, and education.

Oxford   New York
Auckland   Cape Town   Dar es Salaam   Hong Kong   Karachi
Kuala Lumpur   Madrid   Melbourne   Mexico City   Nairobi
New Delhi   Shanghai   Taipei   Toronto

With offices in
Argentina   Austria   Brazil   Chile   Czech Republic   France   Greece
Guatemala   Hungary   Italy   Japan   Poland   Portugal   Singapore
South Korea   Switzerland   Thailand   Turkey   Ukraine   Vietnam

Copyright © 2010 by Luke Timothy Johnson

Published by Oxford University Press, Inc.
198 Madison Avenue, New York, NY 10016

www.oup.com

Oxford is a registered trademark of Oxford University Press

Library of Congress Cataloging-in-Publication Data
Johnson, Luke Timothy.
The New Testament : a very short introduction
/ Luke Timothy Johnson.
p. cm. – (Very short introductions ; 229)
Includes bibliographical references and index.
ISBN 978-0-19-973570-9
1. Bible. N.T.—Introductions.   I. Title.
BS1140.3.J64 2010
225.6'1—dc22
2009038823

5 7 9 8 6 4

Printed in Great Britain
by Ashford Colour Press Ltd., Gosport, Hants.
on acid-free paper

*To students—past, present,
and future*

Acknowledgments

The author is grateful for the permission to use digital images provided by the Pitts Theological Library in the Candler School of Theology at Emory University, is appreciative for the technical assistance given by Richard Manly Adams, Jr., is glad to have had the patient support of Nancy Toff and the staff of Oxford University Press, and is stunned by the good fortune of sharing life's joys and sorrows with his wife, Joy.

The New Testament translations for direct citations are drawn from the New Revised Standard Version and the New American Bible as modified by the author.

Contents

List of illustrations

Chapter 1

Approaching the New Testament

The twenty-seven slender compositions of the New Testament were written in the ordinary Greek (*Koine*) of the early Roman Empire. Leaders of the new cult that arose in Palestine after the death of Jesus and spread explosively across the Mediterranean world in the last part of the first century CE wrote letters to newly formed communities, and twenty-one of them are preserved. Four narratives concerning Jesus (the Gospels), another concerning the movement's first expansion (Acts of the Apostles), and an intense visionary composition (Revelation) were also written over the last three decades of the first century and complete the collection.

The religious and cultural impact of this tiny assemblage of writings is out of proportion to its length, the circumstances of its composition, and its literary merit. As the Christian religion gained a more decisive identity in the mid-second century, these twenty-seven compositions became its official collection (or canon) of sacred writings and, together with the Greek translation of the Hebrew Bible, became the Christian Bible, or Holy Scripture.

From that point on, the New Testament lost much of its human and historical character. For Christian believers, it was God's inspired word, divine revelation, the definitive sourcebook for theology and morality. For despisers of Christianity, the New

1

Testament—above all the letters of Paul—represented all the intellectually and spiritually repressive tendencies they disliked in the religion that had, through the accident of imperial appropriation, become the dominant cultural force of Europe and the world that European colonization shaped.

Three kinds of readers can profit from a very short introduction to the New Testament. Christians can use a fresh look at the compositions they usually engage through acts of piety, and can discover in them both an alarming complexity and a comforting humanity.

Despisers of Christianity likewise deserve an appreciation of these writings unencumbered by the weight of theological and cultural significance. They may be surprised both by the New Testament's variety of viewpoints and generosity of spirit.

For those who already have strong views concerning the New Testament, this book can serve less as an introduction than as a reorientation. But there are other readers who, in increasing numbers, simply have never read the New Testament, have not experienced it as a cultural force in their lives, and have little notion of what has made its compositions controversial or even interesting. They can learn what the excitement has been about.

Potential readers in all three categories should be aware that a completely neutral introduction to the New Testament is impossible, probably not even desirable. But fairness to readers requires that any introduction be clear about the way it approaches the subject. This very short introduction recognizes and engages four distinct dimensions of the earliest Christian writings.

Anthropological dimension

The term "anthropological" indicates that the New Testament compositions were written by human beings, a fact candidly acknowledged by the writings themselves: the Gospels are "according to" Matthew and Mark and Luke and John; it is "Paul the Apostle" who writes to local assemblies. The present introduction does not take divine causality into account, either with respect to the birth of the Christian movement or for the composition of these writings. Divine agency is not thereby denied, simply not computed.

Because they were written by real human beings of the first-century Mediterranean world, the New Testament compositions are limited in their perceptions of the world, of social situations, and even of the divine will, as all human productions necessarily are. Readers are therefore not surprised to find a diversity of such perceptions and even disagreement among them. All human witness, after all, is specific, embodied, perspectival, limited. But if the New Testament compositions are fully human creations rather than the passive product of divine intervention, neither are they merely the result of psychological impulses or social dynamics. In all their particular and partial character, they represent human creativity.

Creativity is found in the process by which early believers interpreted their experience through the symbols made available to them by their culture. The earliest Christian writings sprang into existence within a compressed period of time and within a highly specific cultural context. They wonderfully illustrate the kind of human behavior that most intrigues those calling themselves cultural anthropologists. Within the framework of a fragile intentional community, the followers of Christ reinterpreted their inherited symbols and in the process produced a new cultural reality. To appreciate the New Testament anthropologically, then, means to appreciate that these compositions emerge from a tension-filled process of human self-interpretation, not after centuries but within decades of the experiences that launched the movement in the first place.

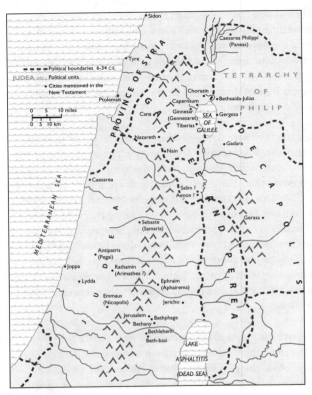

1. Map of Palestine.

Historical dimension

Readers who instinctively approach the New Testament
compositions as timeless truth especially need the reminder
that they speak from and to historical and social situations
of first-century Greco-Roman and Jewish life. Anthropology
acknowledges that these writings involved a human process
of interpretation; history recognizes that such interpretation
happened in the specific social realities of the first-century

4

Mediterranean world. Among them is the intractable fact of language. The New Testament is written in first-century Greek: diction, grammar, and syntax are not subject to the whim of readers. Writings can say only what the *Koine* of that time allows them to say. The only truly responsible reading of the New Testament, consequently, is one based on the Greek text in its historical specificity.

The historical dimension includes the New Testament's "symbolic world," a term that is shorthand for the complex combinations of social structures, dynamics, and symbols within which the first Christians lived, whether they had entered the movement directly from the dominant Gentile (Greco-Roman) culture or from Judaism. Archaeological discoveries of the past two centuries have given impetus to an unparalleled growth in knowledge of the historical context of the New Testament, enabling a fuller and more responsible reading of these ancient texts.

Finally, the New Testament compositions themselves serve as sources for the effort to historically reconstruct the ministry of Jesus, the birth and expansion of the messianic movement, and the particular historical circumstances and rhetorical goals of the respective New Testament compositions. The quest for such historical reconstruction has been a prime motivation for scholarly analysis of the New Testament since the mid-nineteenth century.

The results have been mixed, in terms of real historical knowledge. The New Testament compositions wonderfully witness to the broad historical/cultural context out of which they were written, but they are both too partial and too prejudiced to satisfy the longings for a full historical record of Christian beginnings.

Literary dimension

The New Testament is an anthology of discrete literary compositions. However much early Christians expressed or interpreted their experience orally, only deliberately shaped literary compositions are available to us.

The compositions do not speak with the same voice or from the same perspective. Each composition should therefore be considered on its own terms, without harmonizing them. Recognition of the distinct compositions is slighted, for example, when one refers generally to "the Gospels," without acknowledging how each narrative renders Jesus' ministry, or to "Paul," without recognizing the impressive variety in the letters attributed to him.

The literary dimension also demands that specific literary genres and styles are taken seriously as the vehicles for expressing meaning. Letters and narratives, for example, make meaning in distinct ways. Since literary genres and modes of rhetoric are, furthermore, those of first-century Mediterranean culture, literary attention demands as well historical awareness.

Religious dimension

Readers who are perfectly willing to acknowledge the anthropological, historical, and literary aspects of the New Testament writings often miss this dimension, partly because it is easily misunderstood. "Religious" is not the same as "theological." The New Testament has certainly been used by Christian theology through the ages, and there are arguably elements of "theology" in some of its compositions.

But theology is best thought of as a disciplined reflection on religious discourse and practice, and such religious discourse and practice is precisely what we find everywhere in these compositions.

Three terms need definition. *Religious experience* is the human response to what is perceived as ultimate power, a response involving mind, body, and will as well as feeling, a response characterized by peculiar intensity, and one that issues an appropriate response. *Religion* is a way of life organized around such experiences and convictions concerning ultimate power, seeking mediation of power through myth, ritual, doctrine, and moral behavior, and often seeking direct access to power through unmediated mystical experience. *Religious discourse* is the entire complex of language used for religious experience and in religious practice: the language of myth and prayer, of exhortation and correction.

The New Testament is religious literature in the most obvious sense that it arises from and is directed toward adherents of a religious movement on its way toward becoming a religion (this does not fully happen until the second century CE). Paul does not write as a personal friend to people in Corinth, but as "an apostle of Christ Jesus" to "the church of God in Corinth." So with all the compositions gathered into this collection; they are the official literature of an organized religious movement.

The New Testament writings are religious also in the sense that the experience of ultimate power, and convictions connected to such experience, and the way of life that should follow from such experiences and convictions form their exclusive subject matter. If a reader misses the profoundly religious character of the New Testament's discourse—remarkable in its world for its intense and tension-filled concentration—then the reader has missed the character of the New Testament altogether.

Chapter 2
The New Testament and history

The Hebrew Bible (known by Christians as the Old Testament) bears witness to historical developments in the Near East over hundreds, even thousands of years. Its writings, composed over an extended period of time, are invaluable sources for the history of Israel as well as for the ancient cultures around it. Archaeology is able to confirm, if not the specifics of the biblical story, much of its world.

The New Testament's relation to history is entirely different. It was written within roughly a fifty-year period (the second half of the first century) and provides only a limited view even of events within its narrow range of preoccupation, namely the story of Jesus, the first stages of the Christian movement, and situations in scattered local assemblies. No outsider notices them before the second century, and Christians left no archaeological evidence of their existence before the late second century.

The four Gospels are notoriously difficult to use as sources for reconstructing the historical Jesus. Their faith perspective, their literary interdependence, and the major and minor disagreements among them make a satisfying account of the events of Jesus' life impossible. Even more difficult is an adequate summary of his teaching or his intentions. While splendid witnesses to and interpretations of the human Jesus, the Gospels are severely limited as historical sources.

Some historical conclusions, to be sure, are possible: Jesus'
existence as a first-century Jew, his crucifixion under Roman
authority, and the movement that arose in his name are all
facts of the highest historical probability. Certain aspects of his
ministry are also historically probable: that he healed sicknesses,
associated with marginal elements of society, spoke in parables,
and proclaimed God's rule with a prophetic urgency. Some
specific events such as his baptism by John can be defended as
historical. All this, however, falls considerably short of a genuine
historical account.

The Acts of the Apostles provides an equally partial and
rhetorically shaped narrative concerning the first Christian
community in Jerusalem and some events in the missionary
activity of Peter and Paul. Because the narrative of Acts connects
in significant ways with larger historical events, it provides the
possibility for a rough chronology of Paul's ministry between ca.
37–64. Concerning some events, Acts and Paul's letters agree in
striking ways.

Even so, only five of the thirteen letters ascribed to Paul can
confidently be dated. Paul's remaining letters, and the twenty-two
other New Testament compositions, are impossible to date with
certainty. Dates conventionally assigned them are based entirely
on scholarly guesses concerning their literary relations and the
situations they address.

Scholarly and popular volumes on the history of Jesus and early
Christianity are therefore not a matter of universal agreement but
of considerable and often bitter controversy, precisely because
they must depend almost entirely on historically unsecured
literary compositions.

The situation is reversed when it comes to the historical context
of the New Testament. Christianity and its earliest compositions
appeared in a time and place for which there is abundant

historical evidence. As a result, readers can gain considerable insight into the first Christian writings by locating them within the social conditions and symbolic meanings of the first-century world. In varying degrees all the New Testament compositions display a mix of four cultural elements.

The first are the deep and persistent patterns of Mediterranean culture that preceded empires and outlasted them. Among them is the importance of the patriarchal household in which authority runs from the top down and submission moves from the bottom up: women have less status than men, children have less status than parents. And at the very bottom of households and empires were the slaves who had no status as persons but only as property.

Among males occupying the plus end of the power spectrum there is everywhere a love of honor and a fear of shame, together with the willingness to compete for more of one and less of the other. The field of competition can vary, involving war, sport, or even virtue, but the point of competition is always honor.

Honor and shame fit perfectly within the social arrangements of patronage: if the patron is the one who provides in a variety of concrete ways for clients, the clients respond by giving praise and honor to benefactors. The concept of "friendship," which assumes equality, or at least reciprocity, among human agents, serves to lubricate the strained joints of such structural imbalance within society: thus clients can be regarded as the patron's "friends."

The social dynamics of patronage, in turn, find religious expression in the dominant Mediterranean religious system of polytheism. Divine power is regarded as distributed among an extended family of personal deities, each of whom could serve as patron to humans and in return receive honor through religious devotion.

2. The Archaic Temple at Corinth, built in about the sixth century BCE, associated with the god Apollo in the Hellenistic and Roman periods.

The second cultural element is Roman rule. Since the late third century BCE, the Roman Republic had extended its effective rule across the Mediterranean world. Jesus was born during the principate of Augustus and was crucified by the Roman prefect Pontius Pilate during the reign of the emperor Tiberius. Throughout the empire's far-flung provinces, Roman power was manifest in its system of roads and law, through its insistent taxation, and above all through the presence of its active legions in garrisons and of its retired soldiers in Roman colonies (such as Corinth and Philippi, to which Paul wrote letters). It is no surprise that Acts makes Paul's arrival in Rome the climax of his account of Christian expansion, or that Paul should write to believers in the capital city of his plans to make them his springboard for a mission to Spain.

The importance of Roman rule can, however, be exaggerated. During the period of its early expansion and of New Testament composition, Christianity scarcely rose to the attention of imperial powers. Rome was sublimely unaware of the parasite that would one day swallow its host. The period of the early empire, moreover, was one in which the Greek language and Greek culture, the third element in the cultural mix, was the unquestioned standard of civilization, even for the imperialist Romans.

Although Rome had conquered the Greeks, the program of Hellenistic civilization that had begun in the fourth century BCE with the conquests of Alexander the Great still dominated the Mediterranean world. Alexander had envisaged a Panhellenic world in which the ideals of classical Athens would embrace the entire known world. The city-state, with its cultural institutions, formed the center of Greek culture. The common language drew peoples together. The practice of religious syncretism gave Greek names to diverse polytheistic systems.

The Greek cultural agenda was aggressive and impressive. The New Testament testifies to the way in which Greek religious ideas and practices, Greek rhetoric, and Greek philosophy formed the basis of a common civilized order. Although the early Christians set themselves against all these Gentile ways, their writings everywhere bear the mark of Greek culture.

Christians rejected Greek ways because they identified themselves with Judaism, the fourth and most important cultural element in the New Testament writings. Jesus and his first followers were Jews, Paul was a Jew, and so far as we can tell, all the New Testament writers were Jewish. Their allegiance was also to Judaism, and the symbols of Judaism were the ones they used above all to interpret their convictions concerning what God had done in Jesus.

In the first century, however, Judaism was more than "the religion of the Bible" surviving in Palestine. It was a lively, complex—and growing—phenomenon across the entire Mediterranean world.

From the perspective of outsiders, Jews were remarkable for their unity and separateness. Certain convictions and practices marked them off from their neighbors. They believed in only one God and considered themselves as that one God's elect people, bound by a covenant of absolute and reciprocal obligations. Among such obligations were the practice of circumcision and the observance of the Sabbath.

The activity of the one God, the story of this people, and most of all, the commandments that spelled out Israel's obligations to God and neighbor, all found expression in the symbolic system known as *Torah*. The term refers first to the collection of Hebrew texts known as *TaNaK* (*Torah, Nebiim, Ketubim*), and then to the ways in which those compositions expanded through interpretation to provide instruction and wisdom to every generation.

Despite their shared allegiance to *Torah*, Jews in the first century were a diverse and sometimes divided people. For centuries, the majority of Jews had lived outside Palestine, first by exile and then by choice. In the diaspora, Jews were relatively free to practice obedience to God apart from the specific social institutions of Palestine.

They could adopt the language and culture of the Greeks, for example, without betraying their own heritage. Scripture was translated into Greek as early as 250 BCE, and for Jews in places like Alexandria, this translation (the *Septuagint*, abbreviated as *LXX*) was as authoritative as the Hebrew original. Alexandrian Jews, indeed, produced an entire literature based on the LXX.

Jews in the Hellenistic diaspora experienced—as all minority populations do—a tension between the desire to assimilate and the desire to remain separate (that is, "holy"). But they could resolve this tension in relative freedom. The empire recognized them as a legitimate and ancient cult. Diaspora Jews even enjoyed distinct privileges.

Some Gentiles were attracted to Judaism and became proselytes (converts) or "God-Fearers"—sympathizers who shared Jewish ideals but resisted circumcision and the full keeping of the commandments. Others resented the Jews for their separateness. They accused them of "misanthropy" and harassed them. Diaspora Jews responded with an apologetic literature that interpreted Judaism in terms Gentiles could understand. In the process, they also gave Hellenistic Judaism a distinct character.

Jews in Palestine experienced greater tensions. A lesson learned from the sixth-century Babylonian exile was that Jewish identity could be secured only by separation from pagan influences. In Palestine, Jewish life involved specific physical realities: the *Torah* was not simply religious commandment, it was the law of the land; the land was to be holy from foreign pollution; the temple was to be a place of pure sacrifice, and a Jewish king would rule over the people in the name of God.

In response to the aggressive cultural agenda of the Greeks, and later, the military occupation by the Romans, Jews in Palestine were divided among themselves concerning the question of how best to show loyalty to God: Should they accommodate as much as possible, or should they resist? And what form should resistance take?

The century that saw Jesus preach in Galilee and be executed in Jerusalem, and that witnessed the rise and spread of a movement calling him "messiah" ("Christ"), was one that also saw Jew pitted against Jew on the question of "the rule of God" and what it required. The Jewish historian Josephus describes competing parties or sects that divided on both religious and political grounds. Pharisee, Sadducee, Essene, Zealot: each had a vision of what God's rule should be.

Josephus also describes a variety of popular resistance movements that led, eventually and fatefully, to the war against Rome (67–70), which climaxed with the destruction of the Temple (70). In such circumstances, the proclamation by Jesus and his followers of a "kingdom of God" could not help but be provocative.

Although the New Testament compositions themselves provide little real history, their pages everywhere express the complex historical realities of the first-century world: the patterns of Mediterranean culture, the power and presence of Roman rule, the pervasive influence of Hellenistic civilization, and the symbolic world of Torah within which the earliest Christians sought to interpret their experience.

Chapter 3
The resurrection experience

The Christ cult was born in the highly visible historical context of first-century Judaism, but the precise manner of its birth remains hidden. Explanations for its sudden appearance—let alone its dramatic growth—are various, ranging from divine intervention to human conspiracy. All explanations must find a basis in our only available source, the writings of the New Testament, and must make sense both of continuity and discontinuity between the ministry of Jesus and the movement that arose in his name.

The Gospels describe Jesus as an itinerant teacher and wonder-worker in Palestine. The letters of Paul, written decades before the Gospels, speak of Christ as the center of urban cult-associations across the empire. How do we get from one to the other? Is the shift from a preacher of the kingdom to an exalted Lord the creation of a repackaging conspiracy by the apostles, the work of a religious genius like Paul, or the result of exposure to Greek mystery cults? Such theories have been tried and found wanting.

The best explanation takes all the evidence into account and, in turn, provides the best explanation for the origin and shape of all the evidence. We seek a cause (or causes) commensurate to two inarguable effects: the birth and rapid spread of a religious movement in the name of Jesus, and the production of compositions within this movement that are all centered on the figure of Jesus. The most reasonable way to determine the cause (or causes) is through close attention to the claims of the compositions themselves, while testing for historical probability.

The Gospels do not support the explanation that during his ministry, Jesus founded the sort of movement that appeared in cities across the empire in the middle of the first century. His ministry lasted only from one to three years and ended with his violent death. His teaching was unsystematic and often indirect. It did not provide the blueprint for a community's life. His gathering of disciples and his choice of the twelve indicates a desire for followers, but those he chose proved unreliable: one betrayed him, another denied him, and the rest abandoned him before his shameful death by crucifixion.

The Gospels—above all the endings of Matthew and Luke and the beginning of Acts—make clear two things: something intervened between Jesus' death and the start of the mission in his name, and the mission had a different character than Jesus' own ministry because of what intervened.

What intervened and what gave shape to the new movement was the claim that Jesus had risen to new life after his death and that his followers had been empowered by his spirit. The birth of the Christian movement is the resurrection experience.

Paul's letters, supplemented by other early letters, provide the best sense of the resurrection experience and its significance. They contain no narrative of a physical resurrection. Only once is a list of witnesses provided (1 Cor 15:3–8). In the earliest compositions, the resurrection is less an event of the past than a reality in the present, a reality that involves both Jesus and his followers. They characteristically speak of the resurrection as the exaltation of Jesus to divine status and, as a result, their own experience of power through the Holy Spirit (see 1 Cor 12:1–11).

3. Gustave Doré, *Road to Emmaus* (1872). In Luke 24:13–35, the resurrected Jesus appears mysteriously to two disciples as they journey from Jerusalem.

So pivotal and provocative is this claim that care must be taken to state it clearly. The texts do not deny that Jesus died; rather, the reality of his death is emphasized. Nor do they identify Jesus' "afterlife" with the memory of his deeds, or words, or ideals within communities. Such forms of memory persist, to be sure, but they do not constitute the claim of resurrection.

The earliest writings do not speak of the resurrection as a resuscitation, but rather as Jesus entering into the life and power of God, as an exaltation (as Psalm 110:1 puts it) to the "right hand" of the Lord, thus earning for himself the acclamation "Jesus is Lord" (1 Cor 12:3). Jesus is not less alive, but more alive; indeed, he has become, in Paul's words, "Life-giving Spirit" (1 Cor 15:45)—he shares the power, unique to God, of giving life to others.

Only such a strong understanding of the resurrection makes sense of the astonishing claims being made by these small communities scattered through the empire, claims that are out of all proportion to their real position in the world. From the start, believers claimed cosmic significance: they had a worldwide mission (Matt 28:19; Acts 1:8); they were to judge the world (1 Cor 6:2); the world belonged to them (1 Cor 3:22–23); their faith triumphed over the world (1 John 5:4).

These claims to cosmic significance, in turn, are linked to statements concerning the believers' present condition. They said they were changed from conditions of slavery, death, and sin, to conditions of freedom, life, and faith (see, e.g., Gal 3—5). The terms used for this transition—salvation, redemption, and reconciliation—all point not to a hope for the future but to a present reality. Believers existed now in a state of peace, reconciliation, and joy. They had dispositions of faith and hope and love, and such dispositions had behavioral expressions.

They now had capacities they formerly lacked. Most spectacularly, some could speak in tongues, others could prophesy, reveal, or heal (see 1 Cor 12—14). At the everyday level, all of them could speak with boldness and bear witness to the good news from God that had touched them (see Acts 3—5).

The basis of all these specific claims is the general one of having received a power from God that enabled everything else (see Acts 3:12–16). The power was not political or economic but spiritual—it touched and transformed the human capacities for knowing and willing. To call it "spiritual" does not suggest it was removed from bodily existence; indeed, the transformation of the individual and social body is one of the most important manifestations of this divine power.

The central symbol for this power is "Holy Spirit": the power experienced by believers comes from God (=Holy) and transforms them in their freedom (=Spirit; see 1 Cor 12:1–3; Rom 8:1–17).

In short, the first Christians claimed that they had been seized by a divine energy field and that the power they experienced came to them from the man who had been crucified under Pontius Pilate in Palestine. The expression for their experience was the Holy Spirit; the confession for their conviction was "Jesus is Lord." For these followers Jesus was indeed the Jewish "Messiah," but the title of "Lord" is far more fundamental and radical (Acts 2:36). Jesus was of significance not only for the Jews but for all humans; indeed, what happened in his exaltation was a change in the very structure of reality.

If the first believers saw themselves, as a result of their divine empowerment, to be in a "new creation" (2 Cor 5:17) and part of a "new humanity" (Eph 2:15), they saw the cause and form for that new reality in Jesus as the "new Adam" (1 Cor 15:45). Jesus as exalted Lord present through the power of the Holy Spirit in the communities gathered in his name is the central experience and conviction of the New Testament compositions.

This is a cause commensurate with the sudden appearance of a religious movement as much discontinuous as continuous with its putative founder. This is also a cause sufficient to account for the production of a literature whose most peculiar feature is an insistence that a man who in the recent past had died violently in Palestine was now in the present even more powerfully alive among his followers.

Chapter 4
The process of interpretation

The proclamation of what God had accomplished in the death and resurrection of Jesus was called by the first believers "the good news" (*euangelion* = "gospel"). It surely must have seemed so to those who experienced the energy field of the Holy Spirit in their lives. But precisely the strength of their experience and conviction concerning the resurrection and the presence of the exalted Christ through the Holy Spirit generated severe problems for human understanding, and demanded of the earliest Christians that they begin the process of interpretation—the results of which are the writings of the New Testament.

The necessity of interpreting

Believers found themselves in a state of cognitive dissonance that required resolution. Sociologists speak of cognitive dissonance as the tension between two ideas, or between an experience and an idea. An idea: parents love their children; an experience: my parents beat me. The mind finds such tension intolerable and seeks to find a way of relieving it.

For the first believers there was an immediate and obvious dissonance concerning themselves—between their experience of divine power and their actual condition in the world. If they had a share in the divine power, why were they still powerless in the face of opposition, why were they among the weak and despised in the world (1 Cor 1:26–31; Heb 10:32–34)? If they experienced the resurrection life through their baptism (Rom 6:1–11), why had some of them grown sick and others died (1 Cor 11:30;1 Thess 4:13)? If they had received the holiness of the Spirit, why was there still sin among them (1 Cor 5:1–13)? If the Spirit they received was God's promise to Israel, why was it found primarily among Gentiles and not among Jews (Acts 28:25–29)? Such discrepancies called out for resolution.

Most of all, the very source of their new power was problematic. Jesus was confessed as Lord, but also as Messiah (Acts 2:36), and both confessions created an immediate cognitive dissonance for Jewish believers. The confession of Jesus as Lord seemed to create "two powers in heaven," which threatened strict Jewish monotheism: how could Jesus be "Lord" if there was only one Lord, the creator of heaven and earth (see 1 Cor 8:4–6)?

Worse was the confession of Jesus as Messiah (= Christ), for it clashed with the symbolic world of Torah. There were various messianic expectations among first-century Jews, but any messiah could be expected to make things better for Jews, to "restore the people." In that respect, Jesus failed; nothing got better for Jews because of Jesus.

Nor was he a righteous Messiah according to the strict tenets of Torah: the Gospels speak of his breaking the sabbath (Mk 2:23—3:6), ignoring purity regulations (Mk 7:1–23), and associating with "sinners" (Lk 7:34; 15:1–3).

Most problematic was the way Jesus died. Paul makes clear that the cross appeared to Gentiles as "foolishness"—it was the manner of death for slaves, not for nobles—and to Jews as a "stumbling block" (1 Cor 1:18–25). Torah seemed to have Jesus' death in mind when it declared, "Cursed be anyone who hangs upon a tree" (see Deut 21:23; Gal 3:13).

The cognitive dissonance here is extreme. Is Jesus the holy one of God, the righteous one who as Lord provides the Holy Spirit? Or is he, because of his crucifixion, cursed by God, both a failed and false Messiah? Before the first believers could proceed to interpret their own story, they urgently needed to come to grips with Jesus' story.

The modes of interpretation

Close analysis of the Gospels as well as the social settings and dynamics of the first Christian assemblies allows a partial reconstruction of the process. It suggests that the memory of Jesus was transmitted orally within groups of disciples for some forty years, and that the written Gospels were literary crystallizations of such traditions selected and shaped within communities.

The memory of Jesus' sayings and deeds was cultivated in specific social settings and practices. For a short time, Jewish followers met in the synagogue with fellow-Jews, and in that setting probably worked out a defense of Jesus' messianic claims (see, for example, Acts 13:13–43). For the most part, however, Christians met in private households (see 1 Cor 16:15–20), where the assembly carried out its common activities.

The practice of preaching was undoubtedly the vehicle for proclaiming "the good news," and it may also have included demonstrations of Jesus' power (his healings) and of his fulfilling prophecies from Torah. Worship settings provided occasions for remembering Jesus—above all the initiation ritual of baptism (1 Cor 6:9–11) and the cultic meal (the "Lord's Supper"; see 1 Cor 11:17–34). Speaking in tongues and prophecy (1 Cor 12–14) likewise provided a means of "remembering" Jesus through spirit-utterance. Finally, the communal practice of reading and teaching stimulated the memory of Jesus' words and deeds, both to legitimate community practice and to provide guidance for its behavior.

Such communal memories were complex, because the one being remembered from the past was also regarded as being powerfully present among them. Thus, the words of Jesus at his last meal are remembered in the context of a community meal at which Jesus is present in the Spirit (1 Cor 11:23); words spoken "in the name of the Lord" by a prophet in the Spirit may recall ones said by Jesus while he was alive, or may be a revelation from the risen Lord, or both (see 1 Cor 7:10). For historians of tradition, this complexity is a problem, but it does not appear to have been one for those living religiously within that living memory.

For the most part, stories and sayings of Jesus were transmitted through discrete units or anecdotes. It is striking that Jesus' exorcisms and healings, for example, fall into set forms: sickness, healing action, result, response. Similarly, many of his sayings appear in recognizable patterns, especially in the stories of his controversies with Jewish authorities. Even Jesus' parables, which are so striking in their crispness and originality, find parallels at the formal level in the parables taught by Jewish teachers.

The Gospels place such passages in different places within their narratives, in different settings, and with distinct framing. The analogy of stringing beads on a string exaggerates but communicates the basic point: the stories come to the evangelists as discrete units and are arranged by them in different combinations. Not every passage in the Gospels falls into such stereotypical forms: stories concerning Jesus' baptism, his transfiguration, and his cleansing of the temple, for example, escape such categorization.

But for the most part, the appearance of the individual units of memory within the Gospels fit the hypothesis that they were communicated orally in community contexts and were both selected and shaped by the continuing experiences of communities. Stories of Jesus in conflict with Jewish leaders, for example, probably reflect the early church's conflicts with rival teachers in formative Judaism (see Mark 2:1–3:6). The memories are also affected by believers' tendency to interpret Jesus in light of the symbols of Torah: stories such as the multiplication of loaves (Mk 6:31–44) and his walking on the water (Mk 6:45–50) clearly evoke Old Testament precedents.

Stories that express Jesus' power through his healings or that communicate his wisdom through parables and aphorisms correspond perfectly to the early church's sense of him as powerful and exalted Lord. They do not create cognitive dissonance and do not require a great effort of interpretation.

The story of Jesus' death

Jesus' death by crucifixion, however, does demand intense interpretation. For the Gentiles, we have seen, it was foolishness, and for Jews it was a stumbling block (1 Cor 1:18–31). Because the first believers were also Jews or Gentiles, the manner of Jesus' death was a challenge to their own understanding as well. It was the part of Jesus' story most requiring interpretation, and all indications suggest that it was the first part of the memory of Jesus to reach a set narrative form.

The term "passion narrative" is used for that part of the four canonical Gospels extending from the Last Supper to Jesus' burial. They have exceptional characteristics. In contrast to the Gospels' episodic character elsewhere, this section is disproportionately lengthy. In contrast to the Gospels' neglect of details concerning time and place, this section is circumstantial and sequential. These passages have the highest degree of agreement among the four Gospels. Taken together, these features suggest that the account of Jesus' death was the first part of the Jesus story to be interpreted and shaped into narrative form.

The process of that shaping is still visible in two elements of the accounts. First is the unflinching recital of the facts that

constituted the scandal: Jesus is betrayed and denied by his
followers (Mk 14:43–52; 66–72); he experiences intense fear (Mk
14:32–42); he is physically abused and mocked (Mk 14:65; 15:16–
20); and he is executed with the most shameful death imaginable
in that world (Mk 15:22–32). Crucifixion combined torture and
asphyxiation. It was the mode of execution that Romans reserved
for slaves and rebels.

The narratives do not gloss over the scandal of the cross, but
they transmute the meaning of the events. Jesus does not die
as a sinner but as a righteous man who gave his life for others
(Mk 14:22–26) in radical obedience to God (14:36). The
transmutation, it is clear, comes about through the process of
rereading the texts of Torah in light of the kind of messiah Jesus
was. Jesus dies in fulfillment of Scripture (Mk 14:27).

Jews of that period did not read as a reference to the Messiah the
strange passage of Isaiah 52—53 that spoke of an innocent servant
who suffered for the sake of others and although righteous bore
their sins. But followers of Jesus did. Jews of that time did not
read as messianic Psalm 22, which portrayed a righteous man
persecuted by the unrighteous as crying out in agony, "My God,
My God, why have you forsaken me," and then being vindicated by
God. But followers of Jesus did.

Through such rereading of Scripture, those who considered
Jesus to be exalted Lord found also the way in which they could
also understand him as Christ, even though his manner of death
seemed to disqualify him from that title. So effective was the
process that already in the mid-50s, Paul could state that "Christ
died for our sins according to the Scripture" (1 Cor 15:3).

The result of the entire process was the literary shaping of the
actual narratives, so that they not only stated how everything
happened "so that Scripture could be fulfilled" (Mk 14:49), but
at the point of highest scandal—the crucifixion itself—Scripture

supplies the actual language (Mk 15:24 = Ps 22:18; Mk 15:29 = Ps 22:8–9; Mk 15:34 = Ps 22:2).

What is dramatically visible in the passion narratives is present less visibly but no less truly in every memory concerning Jesus. Believers remember him as one who is still present among them because of the resurrection. Their memory of him is selected and shaped by the continuing experience of the community. And their memory of him is clothed with the garments of Torah, ensuring that Jesus is understood to be not only exalted Lord but also Messiah.

Chapter 5
Literary forms

The Christian movement was also intensely literary from the beginning. During the same time period that saw the memory of Jesus selected and shaped through oral transmission (40–65 CE), we can date the earliest Christian literary compositions, the beginning of what became a prodigious literary production. The writings included in the New Testament are but a selection from the earliest literary efforts and bear witness to a wider compositional activity.

Even though they were written from within a religious movement, the compositions gathered into the New Testament were not intended to be sacred texts that express eternal truths. They were written to address the real situations of specific readers. They made use of inexpensive papyri rather than the parchment or vellum used for Torah scrolls. The recent invention of the codex— the precursor of the book—enabled the cheap and convenient distribution of such writings.

Nevertheless, the production of literature alerts us to three aspects of early Christianity. First, its leaders were literate and assumed a significant level of literacy among their readers. Ancient literature was read aloud, to be sure, so that "reading" was an oral performance more than a private practice. Second, the movement had enough material resources to enable the composition and distribution of literary works. Networks of communication and hospitality provided the context within which literature was sent and received. Third, Christians expressed their distinctive religious convictions by means of the conventional forms of rhetoric in the first-century Mediterranean world.

Communication through letters

The earliest literary expression took the form of the letter, a natural and available vehicle for that age. The excellent system of roads and multiple courier systems made rapid communication through letters possible. Senators and philosophers alike carried on extensive correspondence. Archaeologists have also discovered letters written by ordinary individuals on matters commercial and personal. So popular was this form of communication that an epistolary form was sometimes given to compositions that began as discourses or treatises.

Twenty-one New Testament compositions bear the label of letter. Thirteen of them have Paul as the ascribed author (Romans, 1 and 2 Corinthians, 1 and 2 Thessalonians, Galatians, Philippians, Philemon, Colossians, Ephesians, 1 and 2 Timothy, and Titus). Seven letters come from other leaders (1, 2, and 3 John, 1 and 2 Peter, Jude, James), and a final letter is anonymous (Hebrews).

We can count also letters embedded in two other writings: in Revelation 2:1—3:21, there are seven letters addressed to local churches in Asia, and Acts 15:23–29 reports a letter written from the apostolic council in Jerusalem to Gentile believers in Antioch, Syria, and Cilicia. Extant letters also allude to other correspondence that has not survived (see, for example, 1 Cor 5:9).

Paul's letters are the earliest extant Christian writings. They were probably the first compositions exchanged and collected by churches. Some literary aspects of these thirteen compositions are clear. For the most part, they follow the conventional forms of ancient letter-writing: the greeting, the body, the farewell. The religious character of Paul's letters is indicated especially by the way in which he expands the greeting to include specifically religious language and in the characteristic passage of thanksgiving (or blessing) that he inserts before the body of the letter. Paul uses the thanksgiving to anticipate major themes of the letter.

Paul's correspondence is occasional: he writes real letters in response to genuine situations among his readers. It is official: Paul writes as an emissary (apostle) of Jesus Christ to communities founded by himself or one of his associates. It is various: his letters range from a note of commendation (Philemon) to a lengthy theological argument (Romans), from the simple (1 Thessalonians) to the complex (Galatians).

Paul's letters are complex in their composition: he uses elements of tradition (ritual, creedal statements, hymns, even a handful of sayings from Jesus). There are also many minds at work in the shaping of his letters: in some, he uses secretaries for dictation, some are co-written, and in some letters there are literary traces of Greco-Roman and Jewish study activities that are carried out by teacher and students. When elements of Diatribe (vigorous fictive dialogue) or Midrash (technical interpretation of Scripture) appear in his letters, it is likely that Paul worked out such passages with his colleagues.

Paul's letters are also rhetorically fashioned. The "personality" that emerges from his letters is not a simple outpouring of personal feeling, but a constructed "character" that uses the conventions of ancient rhetoric. Far from spontaneous scribblings, his letters are carefully composed. They are instruments of persuasion in which Paul employs the ancient arguments from reason (*logos*), feeling (*pathos*) and character (*ethos*). They reveal the ancient rhetorical ideal of *prosopopoiia*, of "writing in character": the literary shaping of the letter and the "Paul" revealed through that shaping is fitted to the social context and religious situation the author addresses.

Historical analysis of the Pauline correspondence has concentrated on three issues. The first is literary integrity: some scholars detect short interpolations in some of Paul's letters; others propose that some letters are actually edited composites that have been stitched together from a series of shorter missives.

The second issue is authenticity: Were all Paul's letters written by him? Since the early nineteenth century, each of Paul's letters has been questioned. Criteria for assessing genuineness include fitting the composition into Paul's ministry and consistency in matters of style, theme, and degree of church organization. A late nineteenth-century consensus was reached that most scholars today accept: seven letters are universally accepted as genuine: Romans, 1 and 2 Corinthians, Galatians, Philippians, 1 Thessalonians, and Philemon.

Concerning three of the letters, scholars continue to debate: 2 Thessalonians, Colossians, Ephesians. In contrast, virtually all scholars regard 1 and 2 Timothy and Titus ("The Pastoral Letters") as inauthentic. They argue that such letters were composed pseudonymously by a "Pauline school" writing in Paul's name. Why were such letters supposed to have been written? In order to direct Paul's teaching in a more conservative direction, scholars who hold this theory note elements in the disputed letters that suggest a more repressive stance, for example, toward women (see 1 Tim 2:8–15).

A consensus so long held begins to look like fact, but in truth, the conventional view of Pauline authorship stands on shaky premises, especially in light of more recent appreciation of the rhetorical character and social origins of Paul's correspondence. It is possible to hold that all the letters ascribed to Paul were actually written during his lifetime and under his authorization, and that their composition involved his school already during the time of his ministry. A decision on authorship certainly affects judgments concerning "Paul's thought," but it ought not to affect a reader's appreciation of the literary or religious character of all the Pauline letters.

The third issue is determining the social and historical situation addressed by the respective letters. Some of Paul's letters are so rich in specific detail that the problems in the communities he addresses are relatively clear (see 1 Corinthians, Galatians). Others point with considerable clarity toward the situation in Paul's ministry that prompts his composition (Romans). But the circumstances addressed by other letters are less clear.

All reconstructions of circumstance are tentative, since they depend on deductions drawn from Paul's statements—the reader encounters his perceptions, rather than the simple "facts." The recovery of the occasion, furthermore, does not exhaust the significance of the composition. The purpose for which Paul wrote Romans was to raise support for his trip to Spain, but the significance of Romans extends far beyond a fund-raising effort.

The other New Testament letters present even greater challenges with respect to locating them historically. Each has its own interpretive challenges. A number of them were probably encyclical letters: they were addressed to a wider readership than a single assembly (Ephesians, James, 1 Peter, 1 John). Some of them also may have originated as sermons delivered orally to a congregation, and then were sent to others in the form of a letter (see Hebrews, 1 Peter, 1 John).

Teaching through narrative

The other major literary form found in the New Testament is the narrative. Four narratives (the Gospels of Matthew, Mark, Luke, and John) trace the story of Jesus from the start of his ministry to his resurrection appearances. Two of them (Matthew and Luke) include brief accounts of Jesus' birth and infancy.

Ancient literature contains narratives concerning heroes (like Alexander the Great) and grand historical events (the Peloponnesian War). But four narratives (all written within a thirty-year span) dedicated to an obscure provincial teacher whose activity lasted at most three years and who died the shameful execution of a criminal is unparalleled.

A confluence of events around the year 70 CE stimulated the composition of narrative Gospels. The Jewish war with Rome exacerbated relations between messianist and nonmessianist Jews, making Christianity an ever-more Gentile religion. The same war led to the destruction of the Jerusalem Temple and the loss of the Jerusalem Christian community. Eyewitnesses to the actual events of Jesus' ministry were also dying. The shift from oral tradition to writing responds to the danger of losing the Jewish roots (and therefore the full meaning) of Jesus' deeds and words.

Compared to other ancient narratives devoted to historical figures, the Gospels are noteworthy most for the features that mark them as arising from an intense religious movement rather than a simple literary impulse. The faith perspective, or more accurately, the resurrection perspective, pervades the accounts of the human Jesus: authors and readers alike consider the figure spoken of in the past to be present among them.

Similarly, the fact that the Gospels gathered, organized, and gave literary shape to oral memories handed on within worshiping communities, gives these narratives a distinct density. Three layers of perception can be found in each passage: the interpretive lens of witnesses who saw and reported the event during the time of Jesus; the use of the event in the life of the church; and the literary purposes of the respective evangelists.

Three of the Gospels (Matthew, Mark, and Luke) have such an intricate combination of similarity and dissimilarity among them that they can be displayed in parallel columns. They are called *Synoptic* since they can be viewed together. They are undoubtedly literarily interdependent, and solving the "Synoptic Problem"—posed by the fact that Matthew and Luke agree with each other when they agree with Mark, and that Matthew and Luke each draw from a shared source (designated by scholars as Q = *Quelle* = "source")—dominated the study of the Gospels in the nineteenth century.

The majority of critical scholars now hold that Mark was the first narrative Gospel composed, and that Matthew and Luke used Mark in composing their own accounts. A minority opinion follows the ancient church tradition that Matthew's was the first Gospel written, but this solution does not account as well for the actual state of the three versions. John's Gospel (known as the Fourth Gospel), in turn, while sharing some traditions with the Synoptic Gospels, is not literarily dependent on them.

The fifth narrative in the New Testament is actually the continuation of the Gospel of Luke. The Acts of the Apostles continues the story begun by Luke's first volume and is manifestly part of the same literary project, so that scholars refer to the two volumes together as "Luke-Acts." Taken as a whole, the two-volume work appears as a form of apologetic history much like those composed among Hellenistic Jews, and displays literary features most like those found in contemporary narratives. The use of a formal prologue to each volume and the command of literary tropes suggest that the author of Luke-Acts sought to bring the Christian movement into the light of the larger Greco-Roman culture.

A final literary form, apocalyptic, is found in the book of Revelation: the author describes his ascent to heaven and reveals the visions that he experiences there. Revelation is distinctive within its genre because of the central role played by the crucified and raised Christ and because of the way in which convictions concerning his death and exaltation reshape all the traditional motifs. But the conventional use of visions, of mystical numbers, of animal and cosmic symbolism mark Revelation as unmistakably an apocalyptic composition.

The letters, narratives, and visionary writing we find in the New Testament correspond in many respects to the literary and rhetorical conventions of their age. But they also show how such conventions were stretched and reshaped by the unusual claims that spurred their authors to write.

Chapter 6
The Synoptic Gospels

The Gospels of Mark, Matthew, and Luke—we know nothing about these authors—bear a distinctive witness to the human Jesus through narratives that place him as a character in the setting of first-century Palestinian Judaism. Their composition, probably between 70 and 85 CE, gives the term "gospel" a new meaning, referring not only to what God did through the death and resurrection of Jesus, but also what Jesus did through the power of God in his deeds and words.

The narratives are literarily interrelated. Matthew and Luke use Mark in the construction of their respective versions. The portrait of Jesus in each contains some historical fact, but is shaped at least as much by the convictions of faith and by the interpretation of Jesus through scriptural symbols. Ordinary readers consider the Jesus found in the Synoptic Gospels as the most historical and lifelike, but his portrait is no less literarily constructed in them than in the Fourth Gospel.

Despite their similarities, each Synoptic Gospel provides a distinctive portrayal of the human Jesus. Mark is more than a source for the other two; it is a witness of considerable power. Matthew and Luke, similarly, are more than enlarged and improved editions of Mark; each has an individual and distinctive perspective on the figure whom they depict. A sense of each

Gospel's distinctive rendering within the same frame of reference can be gained by observing the portrayal of Jesus and his disciples in each.

The choice of Jesus as a focus should be obvious: the human ministry of the one now worshiped as exalted Lord commands automatic attention. The choice of the disciples is natural because those in the early church desiring to be "students" (*mathētai*) of the Messiah would identify with those earlier followers. The image of Jesus and the disciples in each narrative serves the narrative purpose of instructing readers within the Christian assembly in the late first century.

Mark: Jesus as mystery of God's rule

Mark's Gospel is probably the first written. It is conventionally dated around 67–70, because the fall of the Temple predicted in chapter 13 is not influenced by the actual destruction of the Jewish sanctuary in the war with Rome. Scholars agree that Mark uses the symbolism of Jewish apocalyptic literature, which arose in the Second-Temple period as a means of resistance to foreign influences through the exercise of literary imagination.

Apocalyptic literature is usually pseudonymous—an ancient hero speaks to the present. Heavenly ascents and visions provide an alternative understanding of history to the oppressed: despite appearances to the contrary, God controls history and will act decisively to save God's people. Apocalypses are heavily coded: they use mystical numbers, personified animals, and cosmic forces as symbols to instruct insiders in this secret knowledge.

Mark 13 is a miniature example of the genre: Jesus speaks to his closest three followers about future events, sketching a scenario of cosmic catastrophe followed by divine rescue by the "Son of Man" coming on the clouds. Mark's use of apocalyptic imagery, however, is not restricted to one chapter; it so pervades his entire narrative that Mark is best read as an apocalyptic drama in the form of a realistic narrative. Mark maintains the insider/outsider irony inherent in the genre: his readers know from the beginning of the story that Jesus is "Messiah" and "Son of God" (1:1), but this truth eludes the human characters in the narrative, who should most have had such "insider" knowledge, namely, Jesus' disciples.

Mark's portrayal of Jesus is thoroughly apocalyptic. This Gospel has no infancy account. Jesus bursts on the scene with his baptism by John—himself an apocalyptic figure—and after his baptism with the Holy Spirit and a sojourn in the wilderness (1:9–12), he conquers the cosmic forces (unclean spirits) that have oppressed humans (1:21–28), to demonstrate that "the rule of God" is breaking into the world through his deeds and words (1:14–15).

Mark emphasizes Jesus' deeds more than his words. Although everyone calls him "teacher" and his stance toward his followers is that of a teacher, Mark reports few of Jesus' sayings: a handful of parables (see 4:1–32), some sharp aphorisms (see 6:4; 7:15), prophetic warnings (13:5–23), and, most clearly, instructions to his disciples on the cost of their commitment to God's rule (see 8:34–38).

Jesus' "new teaching" (1:27) is a matter of power. Jesus heals (1:29–34), drives out demons (5:1–20), stills a storm-driven sea (4:35–40), feeds a multitude with a handful of loaves (6:34–44), and walks on the water (6:45–52). Both followers and opponents ask, "who is this?" (4:41)—a question whose answer Mark's readers already know.

Mark's portrayal of Jesus is more complex than that of a simple wonder-worker. Jesus appears to want to keep his identity as Messiah a secret (3:12; 9:9). More startling, this powerful miracle worker is destined to suffer and die at the hands of his human opponents. Critical to Mark's portrayal, then, is Jesus' teaching to his disciples—through formal predictions of his passion (8:31–32;

38

4. Gustave Doré, *Jesus Preaching in the Synagogue* (1872). Luke 4:16–32 describes Jesus' announcement of his prophetic mission.

9:31; 10:33–34)—that his identity as "Son of man" will be revealed not only in his glorious future (see 13:26), but especially in his present path of suffering. The Son of man "did not come to be served but to serve and to give his life as a ransom for many" (10:45). The passion predictions prepare the disciples—and above all Mark's readers—to understand the significance of Jesus' scandalous death.

Mark's version of the passion is the earliest extant and shows how the scandal was transformed through interpretation: what appears externally to be the failure of the Messiah is the most powerful demonstration of God's rule at work in the world. The weakness of the human Jesus displays God's power.

Mark's Jesus, therefore, is neither straightforward nor simple. He is, rather, deeply paradoxical: the conqueror of demons submits to the tyranny of his human opponents. Through his death, God inaugurates his rule among humans. The resurrection of Jesus—intimated in the three predictions of his suffering, and displayed momentarily in the moment of his transfiguration (9:2-8)—makes the Jesus story a comedy rather than a tragedy, and it makes Mark's rendering of Jesus a teaching about power manifest in weakness.

The negative portrayal of Jesus' followers in Mark is at first shocking. Figures like Peter, James, and John were, after all, leaders and heroes within the early Christian movement (see, e.g., Gal 2:9-10), candidates for admiration and imitation. Mark's narrative, however, makes them inadequate bumblers.

This negative portrayal is all the stronger because of the way Mark focuses his narrative on the drama of discipleship. Jesus' opponents are also important, for they represent in the human realm the cosmic forces against which he battles (see 3:20-30). But the disciples were chosen by Jesus precisely to extend his activity and to "be with him" as companions in his apocalyptic struggle (3:13-15).

The disciples are inadequate first because of their stupidity. Mark ironically twists the apocalyptic theme of the "insider." They should grasp Jesus' parables and understand his identity (4:10-12). Instead, they repeatedly misunderstand even the clearest and nonparabolic of Jesus' sayings (7:6-23; 8:14-21). They are equally obtuse concerning his identity. Peter catches a glimpse of Jesus' role as Messiah (8:27–29), but immediately misunderstands the entailments of that recognition (8:32–33). With John and James, he responds to Jesus' increasingly explicit predictions concerning his destiny with distorted understandings of discipleship, regarding it as a matter of personal authority and prestige, rather than humble service (9:34, 38; 10:13, 35–37). Jesus' teaching on discipleship on the road to his own death is pointedly in contrast to his befuddled followers (9:39–50; 10:14, 42–45).

The disciples' lack of understanding might be forgiven. Mark's Jesus, after all, is indeed paradoxical and puzzling. More serious is their lack of loyalty. Jesus had chosen them to be "with him," and his teaching made clear that discipleship meant imitating his distinctive way of being Messiah, suffering for others. When Jesus enters Jerusalem, the place of his Jewish and Roman enemies, the disciples quickly fall away from the excitement caused by Jesus' symbolic entry into the city as Messiah (11:1–11).

Jesus' prophetic gesture in the temple (11:15–19) generates more explicit opposition and a plot to kill him by legal execution (11:18; 14:1). As this plot unfolds, one of his disciples (Judas) collaborates in the plot (14:10–11). His three closest followers fall asleep rather than watch during Jesus' crisis of confidence (14:32–42). Peter denies Jesus publicly three times (14:66–72). When Jesus is arrested, all of them flee (14:50). Mark takes special note of a young man who fled from the scene naked, leaving his garment behind (14:51–52). The teacher is abandoned by all his students.

Mark's carefully constructed narrative intends to instruct his readers through the portrayal of the paradoxical Jesus and his failed disciples. The lesson is stated plainly at the scene of transfiguration, when Peter characteristically blurts out inappropriately at the sight of Jesus in glory (9:5), and a voice comes from the cloud, instructing the disciples (and the readers), "This is my beloved son. Listen to him" (9:7). Mark's readers are not to look to the disciples for emulation, but to Jesus for imitation.

Although Mark's Gospel lacks any explicit appearance of the resurrected Jesus, his entire narrative is suffused with the perspective of faith in him as the exalted Lord. And although the shorter (and undoubtedly original) ending of Mark's Gospel appears to end in one more failure—the women depart, telling no one because of their fear (16:8)—the basis for hope is found earlier in the passage. The messenger at the empty tomb tells them that Jesus has been raised. They are told to "tell his disciples and Peter, 'He is going before you into Galilee; there you will see him, as he told you'" (16:7).

Although the women do not speak the message, the readers receive it and know that Peter and the other early followers were restored to fellowship with the risen Lord. Careful readers recognize the messenger at the tomb. He is described by Mark as "a young man sitting at the right side, clothed in a white robe" (16:5). Mark wants readers to understand that the young man who fled naked (14:51) is already restored, as the first human witness to the resurrection. Mark's Gospel ends not in despair but in hope.

Matthew: Jesus the teacher of the Church

There are two reasons why Matthew's Gospel is usually dated around 85 CE. First, some time is required for Mark's Gospel to circulate and be edited by the author of Matthew. Second, Matthew's editing points to a social setting of conversation and conflict between the Matthean community and formative Judaism—a situation that best fits the period after the destruction of the Temple (in 70 CE).

Matthew edits Mark carefully. He respects Mark's basic plotline and emphases, while he corrects and compresses Mark's more diffuse narrative style and adds substantial amounts of new material. His narrative additions appear most visibly at the beginning and end. By adding a genealogy tracing Jesus back to Abraham (Matt 1:1–17) and an account of his infancy that echoes the Exodus (2:1–23), Matthew connects Jesus explicitly to the story of Israel. By adding to the end of his narrative a resurrection appearance at which Jesus commissions the remaining apostles to baptize and "make disciples of all nations...teaching them to observe all that I have commanded you," promising to be with them until the completion of the age (28:19–20), Matthew connects Jesus explicitly to the life of the church.

Matthew's most substantive additions are sayings that he takes either from a source he shares with Luke (Q), or from a source distinctive to him. Matthew organizes this great collection of sayings into discrete "sermons" that are both internally organized and thematically distributed. The most famous is the Sermon on the Mount in Matthew 5–7. It is not a sermon delivered as such by Jesus, but one constructed by the evangelist—note that Luke's parallel "sermon" is different in location, length, and substance (see Luke 6:20–49).

Matthew's Gospel is therefore not only longer than Mark's (twenty-eight chapters compared to sixteen) but seems even longer than it is because of the way Matthew has compressed the narrative and has added these sermons. Following the plot of Matthew is difficult because the narrative is so frequently interrupted by Jesus' teaching. Although Mark constantly calls Jesus teacher, Matthew portrays Jesus as teacher in speech and not merely in action.

In the sermon of chapters 5–7, Jesus defines the conditions of life within God's rule; in chapter 10 he provides instructions for mission; in chapter 13 he construes God's rule in terms of parables; in chapter 18 he addresses life within the assembly; in chapter 23 he attacks the rival teachers within Judaism, the scribes and Pharisees; and in chapters 24–25 he provides an extensive teaching on the end-time. It is no accident that Matthew's Gospel was later regarded as the "Gospel of the Church," since its compendiousness and its catechetical emphasis made it particularly useful for preaching and teaching.

Jesus' polemic against scribes and Pharisees in 23:1–39 is distinctive to Matthew, and suggests that the Matthean church saw itself as a school that was in competition with the form of Judaism that survived the destruction of the Temple and formed classical Judaism. This tradition carried forward the convictions of the Pharisees, who considered Torah to be the necessary and adequate framework for living righteously before God, and used the interpretive expertise of the scribes to make the commandments of God flexibly applicable to changing circumstances.

This form of Judaism emerged after the year 70 with Christianity as the rival claimant to the heritage of Israel. The more Christians argued in the context of the synagogue that Jesus was the Messiah, and proclaimed him as "Lord," the more non-Messianist Jews found it impossible to associate with them. Jews eventually fashioned the *birkat ha minim* ("blessing against heretics"), a form of prayer that made it impossible for Christians to share any longer in the synagogue worship.

The shape of Matthew's Gospel suggests that it was composed in the context of this rivalry between those who followed Jesus as teacher and Lord, and those who followed Moses and the interpretation of the Pharisees. Matthew opens up Mark's tight focus on discipleship to a wider context involving the struggle of the church to define itself with respect to a more dominant form of Judaism.

Matthew's portrayal of Jesus fits this context. As in Mark's Gospel, Jesus is Son of Man and Son of God. But his portrait is shaped literarily in terms of Torah. As Jesus is the cause of separation between rival religious communities, so does he become the point around which the separated group organizes its symbols—precisely the ones central to the dominant Jewish party.

Matthew demonstrates first that Jesus fulfills Torah. The specific technique he uses is the citation of specific texts from Scripture introduced by a stereotyped formula, "this happened in order to fulfill" (the cited text; see, e.g., Matt 1:22; 2:5). Such explicit interpretive interruption provides in effect an authorial commentary on the story: the reader is instructed to view the events of Jesus' birth, infancy, ministry, suffering, and death—even the death of his betrayer, Judas (27:3-10)—as specifically predicted by prophecy. Every moment of Jesus' existence is clothed with the texts of Torah.

Matthew also portrays Jesus as the messianic interpreter of Torah. The Sermon on the Mount makes the theme explicit. Matthew uses scriptural citations to interpret the infancy and then the baptism of Jesus as echoing the career of Moses, who led the people out of bondage (see especially 1:15). Then, when Jesus sits on the mountain to teach his disciples (5:1-2), his relationship to Torah revealed by Moses is made explicit: he has come not to annul but to fulfill Torah. The righteousness he demands of followers is not less, but more than that demanded by the Law (5:17-20).

In a series of antitheses—"you have heard it said, but I say to you" (5:21-48)—Matthew shows how Jesus' interpretation of Torah yields a greater righteousness "than that of the scribes and the Pharisees" (the rival Jewish teachers). Throughout his narrative, Matthew shows Jesus definitively interpreting the true meaning of Torah. Thus, when he is criticized by the Pharisees for eating with taxcollectors and sinners, Matthew has Jesus respond, "Go and learn what this means: 'I desire mercy and not sacrifice'" (9:13; see Hos 6:6).

By means of allusion, Matthew even suggests that Jesus is the personification of Torah. To grasp the point, it is necessary to recognize some of the characteristic ways in which the rabbis (Jewish teachers) spoke about Torah. They said that Torah was eternal, existing in the mind of God before it was revealed on Mount Sinai, and enduring forever. Torah was wisdom and the fulfillment of Torah's commands. The study of Torah was as righteous as performing sacrifices in the Temple, and the reason for the sabbath rest. To become Jewish was to take on the yoke of Torah. The divine presence (*Shekinah*) rested on those who studied Torah.

Matthew, in turn, has Jesus associate himself with wisdom (11:19) and declare himself greater than the Temple (12:6). Jesus summons those heavily burdened to take on his "yoke" so he could give them "rest" (11:29–30). The resurrected Jesus declares that he will be with his followers forever (28:20), and he tells them, "where two or three are gathered together in my name, there am I in the midst of them" (18:20). In Matthew's Gospel, Jesus is the medium of the divine presence. Matthew's presentation of Jesus lacks Mark's ironic edge, but in its own right is powerful and metaphorically rich.

Matthew's depiction of the disciples corresponds to his characterization of Jesus. They are truly insiders, who have "knowledge of the mysteries of the kingdom of heaven" (13:11). This view is signaled to the reader by the careful way in which Matthew has edited Mark's use of the titles "teacher" and "Lord." Mark has all characters designate Jesus as teacher, while he is called "Lord" particularly by those in need of healing (Mk 6:28). Matthew, in contrast, uses these designations as a way of indicating insiders and outsiders. Only outsiders—above all scribes and Pharisees—call Jesus "teacher" or "rabbi"; to them, he is merely another human teacher (see 19:16; 22:16).

Insiders, however, recognize Jesus as the risen one to whom has been given "all power in heaven and on earth" (28:19).

Throughout his narrative, Matthew has insiders designate Jesus as "Lord" (see 15:28; 16:22), the title that indicates his exalted status as the resurrected one who is "with them" always (28:20). The exception proves the rule. At the Last Supper, the other disciples respond to Jesus' prediction that one would betray him by asking, "Surely it is not I, Lord?" (26:22). But Judas, his betrayer, asks, "Surely it is not I, Rabbi?" (26:25). When Judas leads the mob to arrest Jesus, his salutation is, "Hail, Rabbi" (26:49).

Matthew's depiction of Jesus' disciples is not uniformly positive. Their moral character shows them to be as flawed as the disciples in Mark: Matthew characteristically has Jesus call them "you of little faith" (6:30; 8:26; 14:31; 16:8) because of their doubt. In Matthew's Gospel, Judas betrays, Peter denies, and the rest of the disciples abandon Jesus in the time of crisis. Peter's denial, indeed, appears as all the more egregious because of the leading role he takes in this Gospel as representative of the other disciples: it is to him, after all, that Jesus entrusts "the keys to the kingdom of heaven" (16:19). Matthew makes a point of noting that when Peter denies Jesus, he does so with an oath ("I do not know the man," 26:72), a form of speech explicitly repudiated by Jesus in the Sermon on the Mount (5:33–37).

The biggest difference in Matthew's depiction of the disciples is that they are more intelligent. When Matthew has Jesus interpret the parable of the sower, he makes clear that understanding "the mysteries of the kingdom of heaven" (13:11) is the key to the fruitful response to the word (13:19, 23). And at the end of his recitation of parables, Jesus asks his disciples, "have you understood all these things?" and they respond, "Yes" (13:51). Matthew then has Jesus respond in a manner that reveals the social and symbolic context of his Gospel: "Then every scribe who has been instructed in the kingdom of heaven is like the head of a household who brings from his storeroom both the new and old" (13:52).

The disciples of Jesus take on the role of the scribes in the rival Pharisaic form of Judaism. They are intelligent because they are assigned the responsibility to teach, and to teach, they must understand. Jesus commissions them at the end of the Gospel, "Go therefore and make disciples of all nations…teaching them to observe all things that I have commanded you; and behold, I am with you always, until the end of the age" (28:20).

Luke-Acts: the prophet and the people

The Gospel of Luke and the Acts of the Apostles appear in the New Testament collection as discrete compositions separated by the Gospel of John. But it has always been recognized that they share the same author—possibly but not demonstrably a companion of Paul (Col 4:14)—and for the past century, it has been broadly acknowledged that they make up the two parts of a single literary composition, which scholars designate as Luke-Acts. Each volume begins with a prologue dedicated to a certain Theophilus, probably the Christian patron who enabled production of the book (Lk 1:1–4; Acts 1:1–5).

Luke's Gospel shares the Synoptic tradition: like Matthew, he uses Mark as a source, and also like Matthew, he draws from a common sayings source (Q), as well as sources of his own. Luke has a copy of Mark's Gospel before him and follows Mark's plotline more faithfully than does Matthew. He changes Mark mainly to achieve greater correctness and clarity. For the same reason, apparently, Luke eliminates most of Mark 6—7, a section that contains repetitions (which Luke dislikes), stories that portray Jesus too much like a magician, and statements that reflect poorly on the disciples. The Gospel presents an expanded and corrected edition of Mark.

Luke inserts the sayings material he gets from Q into his narrative in a more subtle manner than Matthew. Rather than injecting sermons, he places Jesus' teaching in biographically convincing settings such as journeys and meals. The sayings material unique to Luke—above all his collection of parables, such as the Good Samaritan and the Prodigal Son (10:29–37; 15:11–32)—are among the most widely recognized and beloved of Jesus' stories.

To accommodate the great amount of new material, Luke needs to create even more space than he had cleared by his "great omission" of Mark's problematic section, so he takes Mark's mention of Jesus' traveling to Jerusalem (Mk 11:1) and opens it up into a ten-chapter "journey narrative" (9:51—19:44), in which Jesus addresses in turn the crowds, his opponents, and his disciples, as he makes his way toward his destiny in Jerusalem.

Using material different from Matthew's, Luke also creates narrative connections to the story of Israel and to the life of the church. Luke's infancy account (Lk 1—2) is fuller than Matthew's (including a story about Jesus as a twelve-year-old boy), and it works with distinct materials. In the standard Christian "nativity story," Luke supplies the inn and the manger, the shepherds and the heavenly chorus; Matthew provides the Magi and the murderous king Herod. More striking, Matthew makes Joseph the leading figure, whereas Luke has Mary play the central role (see 1:26–56).

Moreover, rather than open his Gospel with a genealogy that traces Jesus back to Abraham, Luke places his genealogy after Jesus' baptism (where Jesus is declared to be God's Son), and traces his lineage all the way back to Adam, the first human in the biblical story (3:23–38). If Matthew opens Mark's drama of discipleship to a larger social context of rivalry with Judaism between messianist and nonmessianist Jews, Luke opens the story to a still large stage, encompassing the entire Mediterranean world.

Luke extends the narrative at the end of his Gospel even further than Matthew does, by including a number of resurrection accounts. His empty-tomb story is shared with Matthew and Mark, but it has a twist (24:1-12). Then, Jesus mysteriously appears to two disciples as they journey outside Jerusalem (24:13-35). He goes unrecognized until he interprets Torah with reference to himself and breaks bread with them; the story clearly means to communicate that the risen Jesus is experienced in the worship of those gathered in his name. Luke includes as well an appearance to the gathered eleven (24:36-49), and, in an ascension scene, Jesus withdraws from them and ascends to heaven (24:50-53). Told with greater detail, the ascension of Jesus is the starting point for the second part of Luke's account (Acts 1:6-12).

The most dramatic narrative extension of Luke's Gospel is the author's addition of another volume. Its short prologue (Acts 1:1-5) indicates that this second volume continues the story of the first, and Luke-Acts makes most sense when it is read as a literary unity. Acts does more than simply continue Luke's earlier story, it provides an authoritative interpretation of his Gospel.

Luke writes about Jesus in a way that points forward to the apostles' later activity in the name of Jesus and makes everything done by the characters in Acts echo what was done by Jesus in the Gospel. In his second volume, Luke was less constrained by traditional material and was freer to follow his literary and theological instincts. Acts therefore is the key to the entire narrative.

Just as Luke extends the story of Jesus out of Palestine into the wider Mediterranean world (Acts 1:8), so he extends the genre of Gospel into history. Luke-Acts is the New Testament composition most fully recognizable as a Hellenistic literary production. It resembles Greco-Roman novels especially in its adventurous set-scenes found in Acts (such as the prison escape in 12:1-19). It also resembles Hellenistic biographies—Jesus and his followers look like philosophers—but it most obviously fits within Hellenistic historiography. Luke "opens up" the Gospel story by noting how the story of Jesus and his followers intersects with rulers and events in Jewish and Roman history (see, for example, Luke 3:1–2 and Acts 18:1–2). At the end of Acts, Paul awaits trial before Caesar while under house arrest in the city of Rome (Acts 28:11–22).

Luke writes as a historian. He has concern for chronology and causality, wanting to show both when and why things happened in a particular order. Like other historians of his time, he employs summaries and speeches to amplify his sometimes meager sources. His summaries of the early life of the church in Acts (2:41–47; 4:32–37) provide a sense of vibrant inner activity. The speeches he places in characters' mouths are his own rhetorical invention. He follows the ideal of "writing in character" in order to express not what was said on a certain occasion but what should have been said, thereby interpreting for his reader the narrative's true significance (see, for example, Acts 2:14–41; 7:2–53).

Ancient histories were rhetorically crafted narratives intended to persuade, making an argument through story. Luke discloses the purpose for his historical endeavor in the prologue to the first volume (Lk 1:1–4). He suggests that he has used previous written sources and has carried out his own careful research among eyewitnesses (Lk 1:1–3).

Most pertinent to his specific purpose, however, are three phrases. First, he writes to his Gentile patron, Theophilus, concerning "the teachings you have received" (1:4), which concern "the events that have been fulfilled among us" (1:1). The topic, then, is God's fidelity to God's promises, not simply in Jesus but "among us," the generation of Luke's readers.

Second, he seeks to provide "assurance" or "certainty" to his readers on these matters. The term *asphaleia* in 1:4 has the sense of certitude rather than of "truth." His statement of purpose suggests that Theophilus and those with him may be experiencing doubts. Third, he proposes, in contrast to his predecessors, to write an account "in orderly sequence" (1:3), suggesting that the order of events recited can address the uncertainty among his Gentile readers.

We can deduce the cause of the uncertainty from the shape of Luke's narrative. From beginning to end, a major theme of the two-volume work is that God wishes to include the Gentiles as well as Jews in the Good News (see Luke 2:32; 3:6; Acts 13:47). Paul declares from his final imprisonment, "this salvation of God has been sent to the Gentiles; they will listen" (Acts 28:28).

The story of salvation to the Gentiles, however, has a shadow, namely the rejection of the message by Jews (Acts 13:46–47; 18:6), which reaches its climax in the same final scene (28:23–27). Such rejection is a problem not only for Jews but also for Gentiles. God's promises were for the Jewish people. If the Jews have not received the promised blessings, God has failed. The god embraced by the Gentiles is therefore a fickle and unfaithful god.

Luke's construction of his narrative "in sequence" seeks to address God's faithfulness, making his work an apologetic for God's ways in history. The key element is his portrayal of the first Christian community in Jerusalem that arises because the Holy Spirit is given to Jewish believers by the exalted Jesus (Acts 2—6). Luke calls this Holy Spirit the "promise" of the Father (Acts 2:39), that makes followers of Jesus the children of Abraham. The first church is the restored Israel.

The Gentile mission, therefore, is not the replacement for a failed Israel, but the expansion and continuation of a faithful Israel. Because Israel was given and received the promise, God is proven to be faithful, and the Gentiles who subsequently place their trust in this God can have "assurance" concerning "the teachings [they] have received" (Lk 1:4).

The Apostle Paul dominates the second half of Acts. He is converted in chapter 9, and his missionary journeys and imprisonments are extensively covered through chapters 13–28. Within Luke's overall project, however, Paul's career does not represent a climax but a denouement: the fundamental plot difficulty has already been resolved when Luke showed God's fidelity extended and received within historic Israel.

5. The harbor at Caesarea Maritima, developed and expanded under Herod the Great.

Two of the literary devices Luke uses in the construction of his story are especially worth noting. The first is his literary use of geography. Luke's story of Jesus moves steadily toward Jerusalem, a point that he makes repeatedly by the careful editing of his sources (see, for example, 4:1–12; 9:31, 51–56). In contrast, the narrative of Acts moves out from Jerusalem (as Jesus prophesies in Acts 1:8) to Judaea and Samaria (Acts 8) and then to the ends of the world (i.e., Rome, 13–28).

This emphasis makes Jerusalem the point of focus, and Luke carefully places the central part of his story—having to do with the passion and death of Jesus, the resurrection and ascension of Jesus, the outpouring of the Holy Spirit, and the early flourishing of the church—all within the bounds of Israel's ancient center. The central part of the story, and the resolution of its plot difficulty, happens in the Jerusalem section.

Luke's second literary emphasis is prophecy. Just as Mark used the symbols of apocalyptic and Matthew used the symbols of Pharisaic Judaism, so does Luke exploit the biblical imagery associated with prophecy. Like Matthew, but less mechanically, he asserts that all of the events in the Messiah's ministry, and in the life of the church, "fulfill" the prophecies spoken by the ancient prophets.

Prophecy also appears in Luke's narrative as a constant literary device. Characters make pronouncements concerning the future that are "fulfilled" through the development of the subsequent narrative. Thus, the risen Jesus announces that his followers will bear witness to him in Jerusalem, Judaea, Samaria, and the ends of the earth (Acts 1:8), and the narrative of Acts "fulfills" that prophecy. Luke is thus able to stitch together disparate parts of his story—especially when prophecies spoken by Jesus are fulfilled in the life of the church (see, for example, Lk 10:11 and Acts 13:51)—and also to portray many of his major characters as prophets.

Luke makes particular use of the imagery associated with the "prophet like Moses" (announced by Deut 18:15 and 34:10–12), whom God would raise up in later times. Moses was the first and greatest of Israel's prophets. He spoke God's word and worked signs and wonders among the people. Luke draws an explicit connection between the resurrection of Jesus and the promise of a prophet like Moses whom God would "raise up" (Acts 3:22).

Stephen's speech before his martyrdom draws the connections even tighter. In Acts 7:17–43, Stephen provides a recital of the

Moses story that falls into three phases: Moses is sent a first time to "visit" his people, but when he intervenes in a quarrel and kills an Egyptian, he is forced to flee (7:23–29); his people "did not understand" that he was their savior (7:25). In his wilderness exile, however, Moses encounters God and is empowered to return a second time to Egypt (7:30–34). In this second sending, his "signs and wonders" lead the people to freedom (7:35–38). But they reject him a second time by turning to idolatry. As a result, the people are sent into exile (7:39–43).

In this story of double-sending and double-rejection, Luke provides the pattern for his two-volume work. In the Gospel, Jesus is the prophet sent by God to the Jews for their salvation (see Lk 7:16). But they do not understand (Lk 23:34), and reject him. When Jesus "goes away" in his death, resurrection, and ascension, however, he is empowered by the Holy Spirit (Acts 2:33). The second volume recounts the second sending of the prophet Jesus to save his people, this time through his apostles. This is the definitive offer, not open to misunderstanding, and its acceptance or rejection will mean the acceptance or rejection of the Jews as part of God's people.

It is no accident, then, that Luke has Peter describe the outpouring of the Holy Spirit on Jesus' followers as a prophetic spirit (Acts 2:17–18) that is demonstrated in signs and wonders (2:19–20). Nor is it an accident that all the protagonists in Acts are described stereotypically in terms reminiscent of the prophet Moses and the prophet Jesus: they all are filled with the Holy Spirit, speak God's word, work powerful signs and wonders among the people. God's second offer of salvation to the Jews is made through the prophetic successors of the prophet Jesus whom God "raised up" by resurrection to address them even more powerfully and convincingly than in his human ministry.

The clues provided by the narrative of Acts enable the reader to better grasp Luke's distinctive portrayal of Jesus and the disciples.

In the Gospel portion, Luke is constrained by his major source (Mark) as well as by the materials he draws from Q and his own sources. Nevertheless, his own vision of Jesus' ministry comes through clearly.

In the Gospel, Jesus is above all the prophet-Messiah. The infancy account (Lk 1—2) shows him to arise from a family of prophets: his uncle Zechariah, his mother, Mary, and above all his cousin John, are all prophetic figures, who speak of the significance of the messiah in terms of the fulfillment of God's promises and the reversal of ordinary human values (see especially the song of Mary in Luke 1:46–55).

Jesus appears as prophet-Messiah at the start of his ministry. Luke moves a story about Jesus visiting his home town from its original place in Mark 6:1–6 and makes it a formal inaugural moment in Jesus' ministry (Lk 4:16–29). Himself full of the Holy Spirit (3:22; 4:1, 14), Jesus reads in his hometown synagogue the words of Isaiah 61:1–2, 58:6, and declares them to be fulfilled in him (4:21). The Spirit of the Lord is upon him, and he is the anointed one, who has been sent out to bring good news to the poor, liberty to captives, sight to the blind, and freedom for the oppressed (Lk 4:14–19). The rejection of his townspeople foreshadows the opposition this prophetic messiah will experience (4:28–30). He will be the sign of contradiction, as Simeon declared of him when he was an infant, "for the fall and rise of many in Israel." (2:34).

As a prophet, Jesus announces "good news for the poor" (6:20) that is also a form of bad news for the rich (6:24). The categories of rich and poor stand, on one side, for all those who are powerful within society, who "sit on thrones" (Lk 1:52), enjoying social and religious privilege, and on the other side, all those who are weak and powerless, who are marginalized within society.

The message of God's reversal is enacted by Jesus' reaching out to women and children and all those who are afflicted with sickness and demonic oppression. Luke's Jesus is a healer of physical ills, but these healings stand for the "restoration of the people," the mending of social alienation. Above all, Luke's Jesus is one who associates with the "tax collectors and sinners," those who are regarded, by the religious experts, as excluded from God's righteousness. It is such as these, above all, whom he calls into fellowship (see 15:1–3).

The posture of "the rich" is enacted by those who oppose Jesus in Luke's narrative, above all the Pharisees and the experts in law (Lk 16:14). They object to his healings, and to his eating and drinking with sinners and tax collectors (15:1–3). Most of all, they object to his making the religious elite a target for his prophetic challenge: they are, says Jesus, approved before humans but not before God (18:9–14). The more Jesus presses his prophetic program, the more it is resisted by his opponents, and in the end, "not understanding" that Jesus brought God's visitation for the peace of the people (see Lk 19:41–44), they stage-manage his arrest and trial before Roman authorities on the charge of sedition and leading the people astray (23:1–5, 18–25). Luke presents Jesus as a public and political figure, a prophet who challenges the status quo in the name of God's vision for the world.

Luke's portrayal of Jesus' disciples is correspondingly positive. They are, after all, to be Jesus' prophetic successors within the narrative of Acts. They are among the sinners who heed Jesus' call (Lk 5:1–11). They leave their possessions to follow him (5:27–32; 18:28–30), thus placing themselves among the poor. They extend Jesus' ministry of healing as the sign of God's rule when they are sent out by him (9:6, 10–11). They join him in his fellowship with the outcast among the people (8:1–3).

Luke does not flinch from portraying the intellectual and moral failures of the disciples. They betray, deny, and abandon Jesus. Yet, because they have such a critical role to play in Luke's second volume, Jesus' chosen disciples are treated within the Gospel as prophets-in-training.

They need to learn above all the countercultural character of leadership within Jesus' movement. As Jesus put himself at the disposal of others without regard to himself, so are they to be leaders who are also servants. The theme is struck several times (see 9:46–48; 12:35–48), but never more impressively than at the Last Supper. Immediately after hearing Jesus interpret the bread and wine of the Passover meal in terms of his impending death for others (22:14–20), the disciples fall into a squabble concerning who among them will be the greatest (22:24). Jesus' reprimand reverses the ordinary perception of leaders: they are not to be powerful patrons, but servants at the disposal of others. The point is made emphatically when Jesus declares simply, "I am among you as the one who serves" (22:25–30).

In the Acts narrative, the disciples appear as the prophetic successors of Jesus, yet it is exclusively by the power of the Holy Spirit that comes to them from Jesus that they are able to act so powerfully (3:11–26). Like Jesus, they are full of the Spirit and speak God's word (4:23–31). Their "signs and wonders" are above all healings that demonstrate the power of the resurrection in the world (3:1–10; 4:33; 5:12–16). Not just those Jesus chose but also Stephen and Philip and Barnabas and Paul share in this Spirit's power and bear a similar witness to what God had done in Christ (see 3:6; 6:5; 8:5; 11:24; 9:17, 28).

The apostles in Acts also carry forward Jesus' social vision in a communal form that is if anything more radical. They leave their possessions, they share all their possessions in common, using them to support the needy in the community (2:41–47; 4:32–37). They eat with sinners; by accepting Gentiles into the faith, and by eating with them without requiring that they be circumcised and observe the law, they extend Jesus' vision of inclusiveness (15:1–35). Finally, they embody Jesus' manner of leadership, finding the perfect expression of leadership in service at table (6:1–7). In Luke's vision of earliest Christianity, it is not only Jesus who is prophetic, but the church is a prophetic presence in the world as well.

Despite their points in common, each of the Synoptic Gospels provides a particular portrayal of Jesus and the disciples. Each displays a different aspect of the reinterpretation of Torah. Each provides unique insights into the social situation of Christians in the first century.

Chapter 7
Paul and his letters

The apostle Paul is, next to Jesus, the most striking and original figure to emerge from the Christian movement. The reasons for Paul's singular importance are clear. He was a founder of communities in Asia Minor and in Greece. He exercised pastoral authority among those communities through personal visits, delegates, and correspondence. He was a key figure in the demographic expansion of the tiny Jewish sect among Gentiles, gaining this Pharisaic Jew the paradoxical title of "Apostle to the Gentiles" (see 1 Tim 2:7). He was the first and arguably the most influential interpreter of the story of Jesus. His letters formed the heart of the collection that would eventually become the canon of the New Testament.

Beneath the obvious facts, however, are a number of difficult questions. The first is seldom asked but is perhaps the most pertinent: Is Paul's historical importance as great as his canonical presence suggests? He clearly dominates the New Testament canon. Add to his thirteen letters the prominent role he plays in the narrative of Acts 9—28, where Paul appears as a heroic witness to Christ.

Does that canonical dominance distort the historical reality? Did everything revolve around him, as so many historical reconstructions have suggested? Or was Peter the truly "indispensable disciple" essential to the movement's initial success and survival? Whatever the historical reality, Paul's place in the canon now demands readers' attention.

A second question concerns Paul's role in shaping earliest Christianity: Was he a religious genius who created, out of his personal experience, a Christ cult that was alien to the preaching of Jesus? Or was he a faithful interpreter of a movement, which he joined after having persecuted it? The most reasonable answer is that Paul did not invent the Christ cult. His letters show that he knew and used traditions (ritual, creedal, hymnic) that preceded him. Still, Paul was a thinker, and he gave his distinctive stamp to these traditions.

Present-day readers are sometimes repelled by what they perceive as Paul's "personality"; indeed, some sophisticated minds (such as Nietzsche's) drew a direct line from Paul's supposed neuroses to the presumed psychopathology of Christianity. But readers do not encounter Paul's personality in his letters so much as his rhetoric. Paul rhetorically constructs the self that best addresses specific audiences and situations. What actually puts many readers off is the fact that Paul is truly a thinker who demands that his readers think. His letters make for harder reading than do the Gospels.

Paul's thinking is marked by a consistent dualism, which is moral rather than cosmological: the contrast between "flesh" and "spirit," for example, is not the split between body and soul, but the difference between selfishness and altruism (Gal 5:16–26). Other polar contrasts appear in his letters: death and life (Rom 6:1–4), darkness and light (1 Thess 5:5), slavery and freedom (Rom 6:15–23), sin and grace (Rom 5:15–21), law and faith (Gal 3:7–29). Paul leaves little gray area. He demands of his readers a choice between the old age and the new, between the old creation and the new.

Less visible is Paul's equally strong commitment to reconciliation. The divisions among humans that in society spell separation are relativized "in Christ," so that the markers of male and female, free and slave, Jew and Gentile lose their absolute character (Gal 3:28) and instead become positions from which humans can contribute to mutual welfare (see Rom 14:1–21).

A final question concerns the sources for Paul's life and thought. With respect to Paul's life, both Acts and his letters must be used, and both must be assessed critically. When the sources disagree, as in the account of Paul's conflict with other leaders in Antioch, his letters should be given preference. For all its selectivity and bias, however, the narrative of Acts remains a necessary if inadequate source for Paul's life and ministry. In fact, it is the remarkable convergence between Acts 16—20 and Paul's letters to the Thessalonians, Corinthians, and Romans that enables historians to date those (and only those) letters with some degree of confidence.

Assessment of Paul's thought, in contrast, must use only his letters. Paul's speeches in Acts are Luke's rhetorical constructions. They are at best an echo of Paul's own voice. Since the authorship of six Pauline letters is disputed, furthermore, and attributed to one or another "school" writing pseudonymously, only seven letters (1 and 2 Corinthians, Romans, Galatians, Philippians, 1 Thessalonians, and Philemon) are usually used to portray Paul's thought. The remaining six are regarded by many scholars either as betrayals or weak imitations of the authentic Paul.

Paul's life

A full biography of Paul is unavailable. Some important elements in his life, though, are clear enough. He participated fully in three aspects of first-century Mediterranean culture. According to Acts 21:28, Paul inherited the status of Roman citizen. If true, the claim suggests a certain social prominence enjoyed by his Jewish family in Tarsus of Cilicia. Paul was also at home in Hellenistic culture. His natural milieu was the city and its games (see 1 Cor 9:24–27), rather than the countryside. He spoke and wrote in

Greek, and his Bible was also in Greek (LXX). He knows the basic tropes of Greco-Roman rhetoric and moral instruction.

Paul's loyalties, however, were entirely Jewish. He calls himself a Pharisee, a member of the sect whose interpretation of Torah was strict but flexible, because they considered the observance of its commandments as the expression of righteousness (see Phil 3:5). Paul's argument in several places uses interpretive principles that later appear among the rabbis—though Paul employs the Greek text rather than Hebrew (see Gal 3–4; Rom 9–11). Paul is, remarkably, both the earliest self-designated Pharisee and the only first-hand witness to Jesus' resurrection (1 Cor 9:1).

In addition to his "jealous" zeal for the observance of Torah (Gal 1:14; Phil 3:6), the fact that Paul singles out for notice in his depiction of his early life is his persecution of the church (Phil 3:6; Gal 1:13; 1 Cor 15:9). The reasons why he sought to extirpate the followers of the way of Jesus are not stated, but they may be inferred from his citation of Deuteronomy 21:23 in Galatians 3:13: "Cursed be everyone who hangs upon the tree." For Paul the fanatic Pharisee, Jesus' crucifixion under Roman authority made clear that he was not the righteous one of God—as the first believers claimed—but one cursed by God.

For the zealous Pharisee, the choice was between this would-be Christ and Torah. For Paul, those who called Jesus Messiah and Lord were blasphemers. He persecuted them because he defended the holiness of Torah.

Paul's life changed course when, by his own account, he encountered Jesus as the risen Lord (Gal 1:11–12; 1 Cor 9:1, 15:8). He understood the encounter as a prophetic call to proclaim to all the nations the good news of what God had done through the crucified and raised Messiah Jesus (Gal 1:15–16). Although the accounts of this experience in Acts (see Acts 9:1–9; 22:6–11; 26:12–18) and in Paul's own letters differ in detail, they agree that

Paul experienced Jesus as resurrected Lord and that he took as his mission the expansion of the Jesus movement to the Gentiles.

6. Gustave Doré, *Conversion of Saul* (1872). Acts 9:3–4 describes the persecutor's encounter with the risen Jesus as a flash of light that struck him to the ground.

Paul changed from a Pharisaic persecutor of the church to its most energetic and passionate apostle. He was convinced that the energy field of the Holy Spirit and the presence of the exalted Lord were present in this community. He expended himself in founding churches, managing his missionary team, and collecting funds. We last see him as a prisoner in Rome (Acts 28:11–31), and he was probably martyred under Nero, sometime between 64 and 68 CE.

Some of the energy that pours out from the pages of Paul's letters derives from the intensity of his personal experience. He is one of the great "turn-about" figures in all of history: he changed from a Pharisee who would not eat with Gentiles to an apostle to the Gentiles for a Lord he formerly considered cursed by God. Paul's thought has a sharp "either-or" quality to it, because he himself was a "before and after" person, one who had lived in one age and was suddenly transported to another, who lived within one frame of reference and then found himself within another.

Another source of the tension in Paul's thought is that he alone among the first Christians so sharply experienced the cognitive dissonance between religious experience and symbolic world. Paul the Pharisee denied Christ in the name of Torah. But once he was Christ's, what should he make of Torah? He was impelled to resolve the tension between religious conviction and sacred text. His way of doing it left a deep impression on the Christian tradition.

The churches founded and tended by Paul experienced him most immediately through his personal presence and the visits of his trusted delegates (such as Timothy and Titus) who delivered Paul's letters to churches, read them aloud, and followed them up with further instruction. Although Paul favored such personal contacts, they were not uniformly successful (see 2 Cor 2:1–11; 13:1–9). The same ambiguity that readers find in his letters was apparently experienced firsthand by his communities as well. They were less than impressed by his presence when he was with them (2 Cor 10:1–2), and had suspicions concerning his behavior when he was away from them (2 Cor 1:17–22).

His letters are now the sole means of access to one of history's most fascinating figures. But when seeking the texture of Paul's thought in his correspondence, it is important above all to remember that these occasional letters were stimulated by specific circumstances and that Paul's rhetoric seeks to respond to those circumstances. Paul's thought, then, is not that of a systematic theologian, but of a pastor who tries to get his readers to think about their lives.

Because his letters are so various, it is a mistake to attempt a synthesis of Paul's thought. It is unlikely that all his convictions found their way into the letters ascribed to him. Each letter, rather, provides a distinct expression of the thoughts Paul considered appropriate to the circumstances. To get some flavor of the range—as well as the consistency—in Paul's manner of expression, it is useful to read more closely two of his undisputedly authentic letters rather than attempt a summary of them all.

1 Corinthians

Paul's two letters to the church in Corinth are of unparalleled importance as a source of information about earliest Christianity. The series of letters Paul wrote from Asia Minor to the Roman colony in Achaia around the year 54 respond to everyday issues in the life of the community. Without them—especially 1 Corinthians—we would know far less than we do about the actual behavior and attitudes of the urban, Gentile followers of a crucified Messiah whom Paul converted and nurtured.

They reveal that from the beginning, Christian communities experienced conflict arising from disagreement and competition. They show how the ideals of an egalitarian sect could be compromised by being located in the social setting of a deeply conventional household. They provide a remarkable example of a new community struggling with issues besetting all intentional communities: the tensions between spontaneity and structure, between freedom and responsibility, between the good of the individual and the good of the group. Finally, they show how Paul functioned as a pastor, above all how he tried to persuade his readers to think in a new fashion about their lives because of the new power they had received.

The evidence of the letter as well as of Acts 18:1–18 confirms that Paul founded the church in Corinth, but left it after a period of some eighteen months. This small group of believers—he calls them "the saints"—was richly endowed with gifts of spirit and speech (1 Cor 1:4–9; 12:1–14:40). The assembly appears to have consisted primarily of Gentiles (see 6:9–11), though it probably included Jewish converts as well (see 10:1–4). Their problems were not due to apathy but to an excess of enthusiasm, a disposition that would be recognized in the Gentile world as *philotimia* (love of honor), expressed through a sense of individual competition on the spiritual level matching their accustomed one at the social level.

First Corinthians provides information concerning community behavior that also suggests the events that triggered Paul's composition and the rhetorical challenge facing him as he wrote. Soon after his departure, conflicts developed among the Corinthians concerning the "everyday matters" of their life together (6:3). Behavioral differences centered on the obvious issues of food and sex (1 Cor 5—10). Belief in a resurrected Lord and in the possession of the Holy Spirit did not automatically lead to one way or another of living in the body. Similarly, there were disagreements concerning the proper order and use of the "spiritual gifts" within worship (1 Cor 11—14).

The Corinthians aligned themselves according to two basic postures. The first was characterized by Paul himself as the "strong" position (8:7; 10:22): it considered the spirit to have given knowledge (8:1), and with knowledge, power, and with power, freedom (8:9). Since liberation took place in the mind and was secure (10:12), the body's behavior was irrelevant. Food and sex were simply material transfers that did not touch the enlightened spirit.

The other position Paul considered as "weak" (8:9; 9:22): it was more fearful and conservative, more aware of the frailty of human freedom, the complexity of life in the body, and the fragility of community integrity. It considered firm rules with respect to food and sex as essential to "holiness," that is, being a distinct people within the world. If one group was overly impressed by the resurrection power, the other tended to underestimate its transformative potential.

The debates led some of the Corinthians to write a letter, asking Paul for his guidance. Precisely that suggestion, however, translated debates into divisions, since other members of the church claimed allegiance to leaders other than Paul, stating, "I am for Cephas" or "I am for Apollos" (1 Cor 1:10). Nevertheless, the letter was written (see 1 Cor 7:1) and was sent to Paul in Ephesus through members of Chloe's household (1:11).

With the letter, they brought fresh gossip: some in the community were acting out sexually—one man living with his mother-in-law (1 Cor 5:1-5) and others (possibly) frequenting prostitutes (6:12–20)—as a way of making their point about freedom. Divisions were so severe that members of the assembly were ignoring their own court and were suing each other in pagan courts over such "everyday matters" (6:1–8). The assembly was quickly breaking apart over the question of whose opinion was "right."

Paul's rhetorical challenge was daunting. He had to assert his authority to morally instruct "as a father" the community he had brought into being (4:15), without falling into the trap of playing the competitive game his readers had set for anyone seeking to be their teacher (3:4).

Read from this perspective, Paul's opening argument in the first four chapters of 1 Corinthians is impressive. Even though he addresses the specific situation of the Corinthian assemblies, he deftly employs the conventions for persuasive rhetoric dealing with conflict, making appeal in a variety of ways for social harmony.

He moves first to deflate their self-importance (4:18). They are saints, but they also need to become holy (1:2). The assembly is not theirs, nor is it Paul's; rather it is God's assembly (1:2). They have nothing to boast of, moreover, because they have nothing that was not given to them as gift by God through Christ (4:7).

Paul then elaborates the implication of their being gifted by the "message of the cross" (1:18), that is, by the crucified Messiah Jesus. He argues that the spirit they had been given has moral implications: they are to live according to the "mind of Christ" (2:6–16): their life in the spirit is to be expressed in cruciform style, in service to the other. The point of their empowerment is not to be competitive for honor, but to collaborate in a shared enterprise.

Paul uses the relationship of himself and Apollos—the other teacher to whom some had appealed—to illustrate the point (3:5–4:6). They have different roles: Paul lays the foundation and Apollos builds on it (3:10–17). But they both understand that the house they build belongs to God. They work together in cooperation rather than in competition—so should the Corinthians work together to "edify" (that is, "build up") the community (3:10). Paul concludes the opening section by asserting his special role as the father of the community. It is his job to teach them moral behavior, and he will carry out that task (4:14–21).

Paul next clears the ground for moral discernment within the community. He demands that a community member living in a state of incest be excommunicated (5:1–13). He rebukes the community as a whole for failing to provide adequate judges to settle issues in its own court and for seeking judgment from outsiders (6:1–8). He challenges the premise that freedom allows behavior such as having sexual relations with prostitutes (6:12–20).

Even in these preliminary responses, Paul shows his central concerns: freedom must be tempered by responsibility, it is better to be in a right relationship with another than to be "right" through judicial decision, and the use of the personal body is constrained by the fact of belonging to a social "body" whose spirit is the risen Christ.

When Paul turns to answering the questions communicated by letter concerning sex and food (7:1), he expresses the same basic conviction. Although he prefers marriage to sexual profligacy (7:1–2), for example, and affirms Jesus' prohibition of divorce (7:10), he does not make marriage absolute. Singleness (as with virgins and widows) is also valuable when placed in service of the Lord (7:8–28, 32–40). The "world in its present form is passing away," he declares (7:31), and the one thing that is absolute is responding to the call of God (7:17–24). The question concerning sex is only how "each one's gift" is used for the sake of others (7:7).

In Paul's discussion of "food sacrificed to idols" in chapters 8–10 he carefully navigates between the polar positions held by his divided readership. Meat markets in cities like Corinth were connected to temples, and common meals involving sacrificial meats were connected to the worship of the many gods of the Gentiles. By eating such food, did Paul's readers collaborate in the evils of polytheism? Paul's "weak" readers, who wanted strong social markers, would have craved kosher regulations imposed on all. The "strong," who emphasized individual enlightenment, empowerment, and freedom, wanted approval for their ability to eat indiscriminately.

At first glance, Paul seems to side totally with the strong (8:1). He refuses to provide food rules for the community as a whole. Indeed, he agrees that since there is only one true God, idols signify nothing and have no power; therefore food offered to them is not tainted (8:4–6). For those thoroughly convinced of this, knowledge does give freedom to eat.

But then, Paul challenges the individualism of his liberal readers. What they do affects others, may in fact lead others to act against their own conscience (8:7). The freedom of the strong, he says, must be conditioned by the care for the weak (8:9–10). It is precisely at this point that he invokes the story of Jesus. The weak brother or sister is one "for whom Christ died" (8:11). The behavior of the strong should emulate Christ's by serving the need of the other rather than clinging to their right (8:13). "Knowledge inflates with pride," Paul declares, but "love builds up [others]" (8:2).

Paul appears to deviate from the topic when he speaks about his own rights as an apostle and how he has given them up for the sake of saving others (9:1–27). In fact, it is not a detour, but the presentation of himself as a moral exemplar. He expects the strong among his readers similarly to put themselves to the task of building up others.

He uses the same rhetorical device in chapter 13, which is widely known as Paul's "Hymn to Love," a passage of such poetic balance and grace that it has had a life of its own. Here again we see Paul speaking in the first person as a means of presenting a personal example. It does not matter what spiritual gifts he possesses; if he does not display love for the other, they are simply empty display (13:1–3, 11–12). The context in this case is Paul's consideration (in chapters 12–14) of the community disagreement concerning which of the "spiritual gifts" should be most valued.

His readers are willing to transpose their competitive urges to the realm of worship. But Paul again seeks to shift their thinking from the status of the individual to the benefit of the community. They are like a body whose many members make a single organic unity, with each member dependent on the other for the thriving of the whole (12:12–21). In the human body, indeed, the less exalted members are often the most necessary (12:22–24). He considers the community as "the body of the messiah" (12:27), since they have "all been given to drink of one spirit" (12:13).

The exercise of spiritual gifts should serve the building up of the community as a whole rather than the puffing up of any individual. In that light, Paul uses his encomium on love (*agape*) in chapter 13 to provide a measure for the use of all gifts. To prefer modes of speech that bring attention to the self is to "think like a child, act like a child" (13:11). Paul urges them to the thinking of adults, meaning that they should think in terms of a good larger than their own (14:20). In the same light, Paul argues that if the gifts are to be ranked, then prophecy, a form of speech that is rational and builds up the assembly, is much to be preferred to an ecstatic and nonrational speech that only "edifies the speaker" (14:1–12).

Paul's lengthy discussion of the resurrection in chapter 15 grounds all of the moral instruction he gave the community in the first fourteen chapters. He says that the Corinthians are being saved by a message about a messiah who died for them and was raised by God (15:1–11). Both parts of that message are essential. They now share in the spirit that comes from his exaltation (15:12–19). But the point of that spirit is their moral transformation. God's total victory over sin and death has not yet been accomplished (15:20–28). There is as yet no total kingdom realized, within which they can sit back as rulers and relax (see 4:8).

The Corinthians have been given the spirit but they have not yet themselves been resurrected. They are still in the body and while living in the body must activate in themselves the pattern of the one who "died for them," through a life of mutual service. While his readers have focused only on the "already" of God's work in Christ's resurrection because they have the gifts of the spirit, Paul reminds them of the "not yet" of the struggle against sin and death (15:50–57). It is to that moral transformation, from "flesh" to "spirit," that Paul summons them (15:30–34).

It is only after devoting all this time to his readers' needs that Paul turns at the end to his own project, which is itself an act of altruism. Paul seeks to involve the Corinthians in the great collection of funds for the impoverished community in Jerusalem (16:1–4). He had committed himself to this effort at the time the leaders in Jerusalem recognized that he was sent by God to the Gentiles (Gal 2:10) and devoted a substantial portion of his active ministry to this effort, which he viewed not only as material support for those in need, but also as a sign of fellowship between his Gentile communities and Jewish believers (see 2 Cor 8–9). Paul wanted the Corinthians to look beyond their internal disputes in order to perform a larger act of reconciliation.

The effort led to unexpected consequences. Already suspicious of Paul and already willing to prefer other leaders to him, the Corinthian church resisted Paul's collection effort, even accusing him and his delegates of financial fraud (2 Cor 12:11–18). As his second (extant) letter to the Corinthians shows, Paul found it necessary to seek reconciliation with a community that was alienated precisely by his grand gesture of reconciliation between Jews and Gentiles (2 Cor 5:11–7:16). In that letter, as in the first, Paul continues to display a remarkable capacity for reaching across places of division and seeking to elevate his readers to a "mind of Christ" larger than one preoccupied by petty rivalries.

Romans

Writing from the city of Corinth in the winter of 57 CE (Rom 16:23), Paul sent to the Christians of Rome his longest extant letter. It had an immediate practical goal connected to Paul's plans for his ministry. But it also had an unparalleled influence on later Christian theology as his most significant statement on the "good news" (gospel) concerning what God had accomplished through the crucified and raised Messiah, Jesus. Romans is universally recognized (with Hebrews) as one of the two longest and greatest theological arguments in the New Testament.

7. Map of Paul's journeys.

The beginning and end of Romans provide enough information concerning Paul's movements and intentions to reconstruct the purpose of the letter. Paul did not found the church in the capital city of the empire, but hopes to visit it (1:10–13). He had wanted to approach them earlier but had been prevented by his work in the east (15:19). Paul was now at a critical point in his mission among the Gentiles. He wanted to preach only where no one had gone before (15:20), and had, in effect, "used up" the East. He planned next to work in the West, specifically in the Roman province of Spain (15:24). He hoped to get the financial support of the Roman church for that expedition (15:24). As Philippi had been Paul's financial patron in the East (Phil 4:15–20), so he wants Rome to be his benefactor in the West.

Paul writes at the moment when he is on the way to Jerusalem with the collection for the believers there that he had taken up among his Gentile churches (Rom 15:25). It turns out that the assemblies in Macedonia and Achaia (Corinth) had followed through on their pledge after all (15:26). After finishing that task, Paul anticipates coming to Rome and then "being sent out" to Spain (15:28). He now sends Phoebe, a deacon of the church in Corinth and Paul's patron, as his agent to Rome, asking the church there to cooperate with her in preparing the way for Paul's planned mission to the West (16:1–4).

Chapter 16 of Romans is, in effect, a recommendation of Phoebe to the Roman believers, together with a remarkable set of greetings to people in Rome whom Paul can greet by name even though he had never been there—an indication of the complexity and far-flung character of the early Christian mission (16:3–23).

Things did not turn out the way Paul hoped. He was arrested in Jerusalem (Acts 21:27–40) and appealed to Caesar (Acts 25:11). He arrived in Rome as a prisoner rather than as an active missionary (Acts 28:11–31). At the time of his writing, though, he had high expectations. He sees his proclamation of the good news about Jesus as the means by which God was at work to bring all humans to salvation. He invites the Romans to share in that work.

If Romans is basically a fund-raising letter, why could Paul not have been content with the first and final chapters, where that intention is adequately expressed? Why such a lengthy and complex argument—the part of Romans that was so valued by later Christians? The answer lies in the logic of apostleship. An apostle is someone sent out on a commission, representing the one who sends him. Emissaries carried letters of recommendation to those receiving them (2 Cor 3:1). But Paul regards himself as sent out as an apostle by God and states emphatically elsewhere that he does not need such letters from churches. His churches are his letter of recommendation, "written not in ink but by the spirit of the living God" (2 Cor 3:2–3).

But now he is asking to be sponsored by a church that does not have personal knowledge of him. In order to support him in his mission, it will need to understand and accept his message. Paul needs, therefore, to send to the Romans not only a letter recommending his field-agent Phoebe, but as well a letter recommending himself as an apostle. He therefore constructs a lengthy argument concerning God's work through his apostle's mission.

Romans is not a systematic presentation of Paul's theology—some of his major themes scarcely appear in this letter. But in the hours of leisure provided by this pause in his activity, Paul brings to a focus some of the thinking he had forged in the letters he wrote to the Galatian churches (concerning faith and the law) and to the Corinthian churches (concerning life for others in the church), and constructs a masterful argument on the way God brings all humans into a right relationship with him through Christ.

In Romans, he tells the story of salvation not by reciting a narrative but by developing a formal argument in the manner of the Hellenistic diatribe. The diatribe takes the form of a fictive dialogue between a speaker and an imagined interlocutor, and has a number of vivid rhetorical elements: the use of direct address and challenge, the asking of rhetorical questions, and questions that are given brusque responses, the employment of polemic and lists of vices and virtues, the citation of authoritative texts.

A diatribe is, however, more than a set of stylistic traits. It makes an argument, and follows a predictable sequence of rhetorical stages. A thesis statement is restated by means of antithesis (the contrary), is expanded, is demonstrated through proofs (logical, exemplary, and experiential), and then is supported through the answering of objections to the position that has been argued. Romans is best understood when it is read as this sort of argument.

Paul states his thesis in 1:16–17. Like all thesis statements, it is appropriately dense. He declares that through the good news that Paul preaches, God's power is at work for the salvation of all people who have faith, Jews first and then Gentiles (1:16). The good news also discloses (reveals) God's righteousness (1:17). The phrase is ambiguous. Righteousness is a quality of God, but it is also something that God brings about among humans. Just as Paul connects salvation to faith ("for all who have faith"), he also stresses the connection of righteousness and faith. He uses the phrase "from faith to faith," making this quality both the source and goal of being rightly related.

But whose faith does Paul have in mind? Clearly, faith is demanded of humans as a response to God's saving action ("for all who have faith"). But whose faith is the source of righteousness? The most obvious candidate is God's fidelity to humans—a constant theme of Torah. It is also possible that he means the human faith of Jesus, intending his quotation from the prophet Habakkuk 2:4, "the one who is righteous by faith will live," to be understood in terms of the resurrection of Jesus, who in his faithful death showed himself righteous.

The actual argument begins with antithesis. Paul describes the wrath of God that is being experienced by humanity apart from the good news (1:18–3:20). This section of Romans has drawn disproportionate attention because of its attack on idolatry and sin—most noticeably, sexual sin. For preachers of hellfire it has been a reliable source of sermons; for critics of Christianity, it has been a proof of religious intolerance.

Paul's target, however, is not the easy one of human frailty but the more dangerous one of human perfidy. Sin is not found in the weakness of the mind or the flesh, but in a disease of the will. It is rebellion of the will against God, the source of all existence, and the assertion of the self as absolute (1:19–23). Thus, Paul condemns the virtuous people who condemn others (2:1–11) and convicts of sin the Jews who use their privileged position to assert superiority to others (3:17–29). Sin—for Paul the opposite of faith (14:23)—is not vice or breaking rules. It is a distorted use of freedom that rejects God's order and therefore distorts all human relations.

Humans do not need more rules or more examples to follow. They need a power that will heal their hearts and enable them to use their freedom appropriately. Paul's thesis, which he restates and expands in 3:21–26, is the good news that God has accomplished just such a reversal, not through "law and prophets" (3:21) but through the life and death of a human being, Jesus. Paul emphasizes that this is a "gift" (or "grace") from God (3:24). Humans can not restore a right relationship with God and others on their own. God established such a right relationship through the sacrificial death of Jesus. Paul uses the language of "expiation" from Torah: the death of Jesus is like the ritual of the Day of Atonement in ancient Israel, effecting reconciliation between God and the people (3:24–25; see Lev 16:12–15).

An aspect of God's gift that is obscured by most translations, however, is that the death of Jesus is not like an animal sacrifice; it is the free and faithful act of a human being. The faith of Jesus is an essential element of his death and therefore of the act through which God put humans in right relationship with himself (3:22–24). On the basis of this act, Paul says, God shows himself to be righteous and to make righteous those who "share the faith of Jesus" (3:26)—a more accurate translation than the usual "the one who has faith in Jesus." The pattern of Jesus' response to God is, for Paul, the pattern for those who have put their faith in the gift that God gave in Jesus.

God reversed human history through an anthropological rather than a textual intervention. In 4:1–25, however, Paul uses the story of Abraham in Genesis to show how the principle of faith is "witnessed to by the law and prophets" (3:21), how the response of faith is available both to Jews and Gentiles (4:1–16), and how faith is always in the God who raises the dead (4:17–25).

For Paul, Jesus is not a new Moses who delivers new teachings. Jesus is, rather, a new Adam, who displays an exact opposite way of being human. Paul develops the contrast in 5:12–21: just as the first human started a history of disobedience toward God, the New Adam, Jesus, begins a new history based on obedience. Such obedience is precisely what Paul means by "faith" (see 1:5, "the obedience that is faith").

But how does this anthropological intervention by God reach other humans? Paul asserts emphatically in 5:1–11 that the gift of God in Christ has in fact reached others, through the empowerment that comes from the Holy Spirit. Jesus' death was an act of love that proved God's love for humans (5:8). It is not an act of love that remains merely formal or distant but has entered into the very place of human freedom, the heart: "The love of God has been poured out into our hearts through the Holy Spirit that has been given to us" (5:5).

As Paul turns in 6:1 to the objections that can be raised to his thesis, we find him asserting in different ways the reality of this gift of love and the power that it brings. The impossibility of continuing in sin (even so that "grace might abound"!) is connected to the pattern of life into which believers have been initiated through their baptism (6:1–11). They died with Christ in order to live in a new way, not in a form of slavery to sin, but in true freedom (6:12–23).

Why was the law not sufficient to make humans righteous (ch. 7)? Because it was merely verbal; it did not change the human heart. Does that mean the law was sin? No, but it revealed sin by making rebellion against God explicit. The commandments of the law were powerless to make humans righteous as long as their hearts were distorted, in the same way that a doctor's prescription is powerless to heal a disease—if the medicine is not actually taken. For Paul, the gift of the spirit is like medicine that is taken: it actually changes humans.

The reality of empowerment through the Holy Spirit is elaborated by chapter 8. Humans are now able to do what "the law, weakened by the flesh" (8:3) was not able to do: keep God's commandments (8:4), discern what is good and do it (8:5–13), pray (8:26–27), and endure suffering (8:18–25). They know that nothing can separate them "from the love of God in Jesus Christ our Lord" (8:39), because they are God's adopted children through Christ (8:14–17).

This triumphant claim, however, leads to a final and most difficult question. If it is the faithful death of Jesus that sets the frame of righteousness, what is the state of those Jews who could not accept Jesus? Are they rejected from God's people? If they are, does this not mean that God's word to them has failed? And if God's promises to his people have failed, is not God himself faithless?

In Romans 9–11, Paul takes up the question that, as a loyal Jew himself, causes him "great sorrow and constant anguish in [his] heart" (9:1–5). In light of his own missionary endeavor that saw more Gentiles than Jews accepting the good news, he seeks to understand God's plan for history and seeks to save God's fidelity to his promises.

These three chapters are Paul's longest sustained exercise in scriptural interpretation. He interprets in the manner of a Pharisee but with dramatically different premises. He rereads Scripture from the perspective that Jesus is the Jewish Messiah and that his fellow Jews have rejected this message. A further premise is that the gift of the Holy Spirit given to humans through the resurrection of Jesus simply *is* the fulfillment of God's promises, and that those who have the Spirit are thereby children of God (see Gal 3).

Paul tackles this most problematic premise first. He argues on the basis of Genesis that membership in Israel is not a matter of physical descent but of promise, or election: Isaac rather than Ishmael, Jacob rather than Esau are the descendents of Abraham according to the promise. God can also extend the promise to new populations: "Those who were not my people I will call 'my people'" (9:25; see Hos 2:23). Paul answers the charge that this is not fair by emphatically asserting the divine sovereignty: "It depends not on man's will or exertion but on God's mercy" (9:16).

In the present time, God's mercy invites into the people Gentiles "who did not strive for righteousness" because they have shown faith in the gift God revealed through the crucified and raised Messiah Jesus (9:30). Most Jews in the present time have stumbled over the scandal of the cross and are not able to accept the "righteousness that comes from God" (10:2–3). Election and exclusion, expansion and contraction are happening now according to scriptural precedent.

Paul finally turns to the question whether God has rejected his people. Paul instinctively answers, "by no means!" (11:1). At the present time, Paul and his fellow-believers in Christ form a remnant people of Israel (11:2–6). As for the majority of Paul's fellow Jews who persist in their "hardness" (11:7), they have stumbled but they have not fallen (11:11). Indeed, their momentary rejection of the Messiah Jesus actually plays a key role in God's plan to form a people out of all nations.

Paul argues that the Jewish rejection of Jesus actually opens the way to the Gentile mission. Paradoxically, the Jews have done a service to Gentiles by enabling the Messiah to be proclaimed to them. But Paul hopes that his fellow Jews will be made jealous by the growth of this people based on faith and will, in the end, receive the good news and be received back fully into the people of the promise, the people of the spirit, the people of faith: "and so all Israel will be saved" (11:26).

Having answered all the objections to his thesis, Paul turns in Romans 12—15 to direct exhortation of his readers concerning the way they are to live in light of the gift they have been given. He emphasizes some of the same points as in 1 Corinthians. His readers are to be transformed in their mind (12:1–2) and to "put on" the Lord Jesus Christ (13:14). That is, their manner of life is to display the dispositions of the Messiah. They are to be humble rather than arrogant. They are to serve the good of the community more than self-interest (12:3–21, 8–10). They are to work out their differences in perspective and practice through attitudes of mutual acceptance (14:1–23). The strong are to bear with the weak rather than seek to please themselves. Everyone should seek to build up the community (15:1–6). At the end of Romans, Paul presents the way in which God has worked among them as the model for the manner of their life together: "welcome one another, therefore, as Christ has welcomed you, for the glory of God" (15:7).

Each of Paul's letters has its own character, but the traits shown in his Corinthian and Roman letters are present in them all. Paul is a religious enthusiast: even his most everyday movements are shaped by an awareness of God's presence and call. He is a theologian: even the most quotidian aspects of life are read from the perspective of a cosmic drama of sin and grace. He is a pastor: even his most soaring thoughts return to the practical implications of life in common. He is a writer: even in translation, it is impossible not to recognize the vigor of his prose. He is a moral teacher: even practical projects provide the occasion for instruction in moral transformation.

Chapter 8
Two hidden treasures

However tempting it is to pay attention only to passages of obvious appeal, such as the Sermon on the Mount, or compositions of obvious importance, such as the Gospels and Paul's letters, serious readers need to be aware that such selectivity means missing powerful if less well-known literary witnesses from earliest Christianity. Some of the gems in the collection are less appreciated in the present, but in the past had considerable influence in shaping Christian consciousness. The anonymous composition known as the Letter to the Hebrews (or simply "Hebrews"), and the Letter of James, invite such attention. They illustrate the diversity found in the New Testament collection. They are also works of real substance.

Hebrews: preaching as theology

In contrast to Paul's letters to the Corinthians and Romans, which can be situated historically with some confidence, the anonymous composition known as Hebrews refuses to answer the most basic questions concerning its circumstances. We do not know the author, the place of composition, or the audience. The best guesswork dates the writing as roughly contemporary to Paul, or at most a decade later. Hebrews appears in the New Testament in much the manner as its own description of the ancient priest Melchizedek, "without father, mother, or ancestry" (Heb 7:3).

Some inferences are allowed by the shape of the composition. It is written in the best Greek found in the New Testament and displays a command of rhetoric that suggests a level of education both in author and readers. The dense use of scriptural citation and allusion points to an immersion in the symbolic world of Torah. There are no genuine epistolary elements; the final greetings appear tacked on (13:23–25). Indeed, the style of the composition is so thoroughly oral that the book of Hebrews probably originated as a sermon that was then written down and sent on to readers.

The composition similarly provides some clues to the circumstances of the addressees. Although the title "to the Hebrews" is added later, there is good reason to suppose that the first audience were ethnically Hellenistic Jews. The author speaks of a "new covenant" (8:13), but never suggests that the "children of Abraham" (3:16) were not part of it. Rather, the author speaks of God speaking to "our fathers" through the prophets, as now God speaks to "us" through a son (1:1–2). The audience was also Christian: the hearers had received baptism and "basic instruction about the Christ" (6:1–4). Some time, in fact, had passed since their initiation into the movement, and their first enthusiasm had waned (10:32–35).

Members of the community were in danger of "falling away" or apostatizing (Heb 6:4–8; 10:35; 12:12–13). They were already neglecting the assemblies (10:25). Their lassitude is connected to their experience of suffering. They were not suffering martyrdom (12:4), but some members of the community were imprisoned, and others had their property taken from them (10:34). Such experiences were sufficiently shaming to make members of a new religious movement rethink their commitment (10:33). Add on to this the mere fact of worshiping one who had died the most shameful death imaginable, that of crucifixion (12:2). Was not the sheer fact of association with such shame a cause of shame? The kind of suffering that arose from and led to the experience of shame led to discouragement and even disaffection.

The speaker therefore had the challenge of persuading his audience to hold fast to their commitment, offering reasons why they should maintain their loyalty. The basic form of his argument is known both among Jews and Greeks. The argument from the lesser to the greater is the "if...then" form of analogy: if such and such is the case in a smaller thing, then (by inference) it must be even more so in this greater thing. This single form of argument runs through the entire composition, giving it rhetorical coherence.

In all analogies, some element remains constant. For Hebrews, it is the one God who constantly speaks to and summons God's people. The element of difference is found in the agents through whom God addresses the people. In the past, God spoke through "the prophets," by which Hebrews means all the mediators between God and Israel, including the angels (1:5–2:2), Moses (3:1–6), and the priests descended from Moses' brother, Aaron (7:1–28). In the present, God speaks to the people through "a Son," namely Jesus Christ. One key to Hebrews' argument, therefore, is demonstrating the superiority of Jesus to God's earlier agents.

The point is scarcely theoretical. The promises of God in the past—the security of the people in their own land, their prosperity and honor—were predicated on loyalty to the one God making the promise (see Deut 28:1—30:20). The threat for disloyalty was equally real: dying in the wilderness rather than reaching the promised land, being sent into exile among the nations rather than staying in the land of promise.

For Hebrews, both the promise and threat connected to Jesus Christ are more powerful because of the supremacy of the Son as God's agent. The promise is not life on the land but life with God (4:1–13). The threat therefore is equally dire: being cut off from the people and missing out on eternal life (6:5–8; 12:25–29). The argument in Hebrews is not simply theological (concerned with the nature of Christ) but eminently practical (concerned with the future of the audience). Its rhetoric therefore alternates exposition and exhortation throughout the sermon, leading to the climactic exposition of 11:1–40 and the climactic exhortation in 12:1–29.

Hebrews highlights two aspects of the symbolic world of the Mediterranean that are less evident in other New Testament writings. The first is a Platonic outlook. By the first century, certain perceptions derived from Plato had widespread though not universal currency, much in the way a "Freudian outlook" appeared in late twentieth-century conversations among those who had never read Freud. This Platonic worldview can be described (over-)simply in terms of a dualism between the material and the ideal, a dualism that has three facets. The first is ontological: the ideal world of forms (the *noumenal*) is more real than the transitory and corruptible realm of material appearances (the *phenomenal*). The second is epistemological: truth is connected to what is real (that is, the realm of spirit), whereas in the realm of bodies, only opinion is possible. The third is axiological: the realm of the ideal is better than the arena of appearances. In short, what is unseen is more real, truer, and better than what is seen.

Among Hellenistic Jews like Philo of Alexandria, such Platonic perceptions governed the reading of Israel's scriptures (in Greek), so that "heaven" could be read as the realm of the ideal, and "earth" as the place of transitory phenomena. Allegorical readings enabled the literal stories about escape from Egypt and deliverance to Canaan, for example, to be understood as the escape from vice and deliverance to virtue, or even escape from physical trammels and deliverance to pure spirit. Such merging of biblical cosmology and Platonic categories is found also in Hebrews. When Christ is exalted to the "right hand of God" (Ps 110:1; Heb 1:13) as Lord, Hebrews understands him to have entered into the realm of eternal life, where there is no longer change. The exaltation of Jesus is a movement from the phenomenal to the noumenal world, a condition more real, truer, and better than his earthly condition. The promise offered by Christ to those who follow him, correspondingly, is a "heavenly homeland" infinitely better than any earthly habitation (11:10, 16; 13:14).

Hebrews also engages the symbolism of the ancient cult— especially the practice of sacrifice—more intensely than other New Testament compositions. They can conceive of Christ's death as a sacrifice (see Rom 3:21–26), but nowhere else is Christ himself pictured as a priest. Hebrews finds the image of the High Priest in the same psalm that speaks of Christ's royal exaltation as Lord (Ps 110:1): "The LORD has sworn and he will not repent: you are a priest forever according to the order of Melchizedek" (Ps. 110:4; see Heb 7:21). By the same exaltation, Jesus is both the King who rules forever and the Priest who offers eternal sacrifice.

Hebrews pulls these elements together to make an argument about Christ that is both ontological and moral. At the ontological level, Christ is the perfect mediator between God and humans (9:15) because he is both divine and human. Hebrews asserts the full divinity of Christ (1:2—2:9), but just as dramatically Christ's full share in humanity (2:10–18). The moral argument, however, indicates that Christ's mediating role is not static but dynamic: as a human being, he learns obedience through the things he suffers, moving progressively into a full maturity as "God's son" (5:7–10) The moment of death, which appears as absolute closure, is in reality a full opening to the divine presence. Christ carries humanity into the presence of God (10:11–21).

The central portion of Hebrews (chs. 5—10) concentrates on the comparison between the ancient sacrificial cult of Israel and the priestly work of Christ. In contrast to the levitical priests who died, Christ lives forever (7:23–25). More significantly, whereas the ancient priests could accomplish only an external, ritual purity, Christ effects the purification of the inner person, the human conscience (9:8–14). Standing in the presence of God,

Christ represents humanity as its priest forever and therefore holds out for his followers the promise of a like share in the divine life.

Hebrews contains plenty of negative admonition concerning the dangers of falling away. Its most powerful exhortation, however, is positive. The author summons readers to respond to the call of God "today as long as it is called 'today'" (3:12–13), to move forward in pilgrimage toward the heavenly homeland that Jesus has already attained (4:1–11), and in comparison to which their loss of material property is negligible. Most dramatically, in 11:1–40, the author calls the roll of all the biblical heroes, who "by faith" remained loyal to God in all circumstances, knowing that their true home was not on earth but in heaven (11:13–16). This throng now stands as a "cloud of witnesses" (12:1) for those the author now exhorts to "keep [their] eyes on Jesus, the leader and perfecter of faith" (12:2), as they make their way through the suffering that brings them to maturity (12:3–13) in the secure hope of reaching the place where Jesus now lives (12:22–24).

Jesus is, in the book of Hebrews, both the cause of salvation and the model of obedient faith. The exemplary character of his faith is shown in the simple line, "for the sake of the joy that lay before him he endured the cross, despising its shame, and has taken his seat at the right of the throne of God" (12:2). The author expects his readers also "go to Jesus outside the camp, bearing the reproach that he bore" in the knowledge that "here we have no lasting city, but we seek the one that is to come" (13:13–14).

James: powerful moral exhortation

This short letter is unlike Hebrews in almost every respect, yet it stands within the New Testament collection as another powerful voice from the first Christian generation. The James to whom the letter is ascribed may well be the one called by Paul "the brother of the Lord" (Gal 1:19), that is, Jesus' sibling (Mk 6:3) who was also a witness to the resurrection (1 Cor 15:7) and exercised authority in the Jerusalem church (Acts 15:13–21; 21:18).

The composition may have begun as a sermon, but by being sent "to the twelve tribes of the dispersion" (James 1:1), it became a circular letter to Jewish believers throughout the Mediterranean world. The Jewish historian Josephus tells us James was martyred in 62 CE (*Antiquities* 20:9), so if the historical James was the author, this letter also is roughly contemporary to Paul.

8. Christoph Weigel, *James of Jerusalem*: leader of the original Christian community and author of a circular letter to Jewish-Christians.

The interpretation of James has consistently been distorted, in fact, by being read with reference to Paul. Paul's insistence that humans are righteous because of faith rather than "works of the law" (ritual observances such as circumcision), and Paul's use of Abraham as an example of such "righteousness by faith" (Gal 2:16; Rom 4:1–25), appears to be directly contradicted by James's insistence that "faith without works is dead" (James 2:20), and his use of Abraham as an example to show that "a person is declared righteous by works and not by faith alone" (2:24). But the contradiction is illusory. Paul contrasts faith and ritual observance; James contrasts verbal profession and action (see James 2:14–19). James and Paul are more in agreement than in disagreement: both insist that belief must be spelled out in behavior.

The distinctiveness of James is due to its unswerving attention to the moral dimension of discipleship. James does not speak about Jesus in the manner of Paul and Hebrews. The composition mentions Jesus Christ only twice (1:1; 2:1) and makes no reference either to the events of Jesus' life or to his death and resurrection. Jesus is present, however, through his words: James uses the sayings of Jesus with some frequency, not by direct citation but through the subtle sort of appropriation and allusion that one might expect in a member of the family who belongs to the same movement (see, e.g., 2:5; 5:12)

Nor is it the case that James lacks theology in the proper sense, that is, language about God. God is creator, lawgiver, savior, judge (1:18; 4:12; 1:21). God approaches people (4:8) and lifts them up (5:15). God enters into friendship with humans (2:23; 4:4). James uses his rich set of propositions about God as warrants for his moral instruction. Because God is above all, the perfect "giver of gifts" (1:17; 4:6) who "gives to all generously and without grudging" (1:5), so are humans to act as givers rather than takers.

James makes use of the entire spectrum of the Scripture, including the tradition of Jewish wisdom literature. James makes wisdom thematic and draws a contrast between the "wisdom from above" that comes from God and leads to peace, and a "wisdom from below" that draws its inspiration from the devil and leads to conflict (3:13–18). James not only talks about wisdom, however; he carries on the tradition of moral instruction found in wisdom writings in the ancient world, providing guidance on proper speech (3:1–12), for example, and perceptions of wealth and poverty (1:9–11; 4:13–17).

James also inherits the prophetic tradition from Torah. Like the prophets, he excoriates those who oppress the poor by withholding their wages (5:1–6) and dragging them into court (2:6). He warns against an arrogance that depends on wealth and reminds his readers of the transitory character of possessions and life itself (4:13–17). He summons readers to conversion from an arrogance that is expressed through envy and competition to a humility that is expressed in cooperation (4:8–10). They must choose between being "friends with God" as was Abraham (2:23) and "friends with the world," as are those who live by the wisdom from below (4:4). There is no middle ground.

Most strikingly, James has a positive view of law. He speaks about the perfect law of liberty (1:25) as applicable to his readers. He does not mean circumcision or ritual observances—the things Paul opposed as "works of the law"—but he has in mind specifically what he terms "the royal law" (perhaps better translated as the "law of the kingdom") found in Leviticus 19:18, "Love your neighbor as yourself." James, like Jesus (in Mk 12:31), and like Paul (in Gal 5:14 and Rom 13:9), finds in this statement the adequate summation of moral disposition (2:8).

James explicates that command by scattering throughout his composition the very expressions of neighbor-love that are found in the original context of Leviticus 19:11–18. Love is not compatible with discrimination based on appearances (2:1–5), slandering a brother or sister (5:9), judging another (4:11), practicing oppression against the poor (5:1–6), or taking false oaths (5:12). James intertwines his statements on law with sayings derived from Jesus. Thus, Leviticus 19:12 forbids swearing falsely in the name of the Lord, but James makes the prohibition of oaths absolute in the same way that Jesus did (Jas 5:12; see Matt 5:33–37).

James also exploits Torah for examples to illustrate the practical "works of faith." Employing a popular metaphor, James exhorts his readers to look as in a mirror into "the perfect law, the law of liberty" (1:25) to see how to become doers of the word that God implanted within them (1:18). He then shows how Abraham exemplified the obedience of faith when he was willing to sacrifice his son, Isaac, and so was declared righteous and a "friend of God" (2:23). Rahab also showed the "work of faith" when she received Israel's spies into her house because she was convinced that they represented "the Lord your God [who] is indeed God in heaven above and earth below" (Josh 2:11; Jas 2:25). Job exemplifies the patience of faith (5:10). And the prophet Elijah, a "human being like us," exemplifies the power of the prayer of faith (5:17).

James shows in 2:1–6 how those professing faith can act inconsistently with that profession. He pictures an assembly shunting a poor person aside, while a wealthy visitor is shown deference. Such behavior is perfectly normal for those who are "friends of the world" (4:4), because the world operates on the basis of appearances and privilege. But the measure of faith is different than that of the world. Alluding to the beatitude of Jesus, "blessed are you poor" (Lk 6:20), James asks, "Has not God chosen the poor in the world to be rich in faith and to be heirs of the kingdom that he has promised to those who love him?" (2:5). Such "double-minded" people have internalized the same oppressive dispositions that have been turned against them: "Are not the rich oppressing you? And do they themselves not haul you off to court?" (2:6).

In 5:12–20, James presents a more positive portrait of the assembly. It speaks the truth simply: "let your 'Yes' be yes and your 'No, no'" (5:12). It does not grumble or lie. Those who are suffering pray; those who are cheerful sing songs of praise (5:13). The assembly does not, as in the earlier vignette, follow the logic of envy and competition, but that of collaboration and gift-giving consistent with faith in a God who gives to all generously and without grudging. The sick within the community are not excluded, but they have the power to summon the elders of the community, who come and attend to them with anointing and prayer (5:13–15). The members of the community confess their sins to each other and pray for one another (5:16). They practice mutual correction, seeking to turn each other from the path of error (5:19–20).

Because James is a form of wisdom that does not concern itself with good manners but only with morals, that pays no attention to sex but much attention to possessions, that addresses not only the fact but also the roots of war and violence (4:1–3), that recognizes the power and the peril of speech, that envisages a community of cooperation as a challenge to a world of competition, it is a witness that is particularly pertinent to readers who ask whether the New Testament writings have anything valuable to say for social ethics.

Chapter 9
Johannine literature

Five compositions in the New Testament collection are associated with the name of John: three letters, the Fourth Gospel, and the book of Revelation. A variety of critical questions gather around these writings. Was there a specific community that produced them? If so, where was it located? Or do these compositions arise from a style of Christianity that was geographically scattered? What was the link between the eponymous founder of this form of Christianity—the "disciple whom Jesus loved" who appears as trustworthy witness in the Gospel of John—and the authorship of this disparate group of writings?

Was there a "Johannine School" whose labors account for the multilayered character of the Fourth Gospel? Can the very real differences among the writings (along with remarkable similarities) best be accounted for by changes in historical circumstances, or by the literary refraction effected by three distinct genres (epistolary, narrative, and apocalyptic)? The basic introductory questions elude clear answers.

There is a manuscript of the Fourth Gospel dating from ca. 110 CE. The persecution reflected in Revelation may have been that of Domitian, ca. 96. The author of Revelation locates himself on the island of Patmos and addresses seven churches in Asia Minor. There are traditions associated with John in Asia Minor. It is not unreasonable, then, to place the production of this literature in late first-century communities in the area of Asia Minor that trace their origin to John, the disciple of Jesus.

The historical setting of the Johannine literature may be uncertain. Its character is not. These writings patently emerge from and bear the marks of deep conflict. In the narrative of the Fourth Gospel, the conflict is external: Jesus is violently resisted by those called simply "the Jews" (Jn 7:1) and he warns his followers, "if the world hates you, realize that it hated me first" (16:18). In the three letters, the conflict is internal, between rival leaders, and between opposing factions within the same community. In Revelation, conflict is both internal (within the seven churches of Asia addressed in chs. 2—3) and external (the oppression against Christians by the Roman Empire).

Conflict is reflected in the sharply dualistic symbolism found in all these compositions. They contrast light and darkness, truth and falsehood, flesh and spirit, life and death, true prophecy and false prophecy, God and Satan. Such polar opposites express the conflict between "us" and "them," with all positive attributes falling in the "us" column and all negative qualities on the "them." The intense insider-outsider outlook expressed by this symbolism is properly designated as sectarian: Johannine Christianity is defined as much by what it opposes as by what it affirms.

The dualistic symbolism of the Johannine writings is organized around the figure of Jesus. In the Fourth Gospel, he is the light of the world (8:12), and the rejection of him places his opponents in darkness (3:18–21). It is because of confessing Jesus that believers are expelled from the synagogue (9:22). In the three letters, conflict over the proper understanding of Jesus divides communities: those who properly confess him live in the truth and the light; those who do not are false prophets and antichrists (2 John 7). In Revelation, witness to Jesus is the spirit of prophecy (Rev 19:10), and such witness is the reason why the saints are persecuted.

Such remarks on social setting, dualistic symbolism, and sectarian outlook are all true enough. They account in part for the peculiar power of these compositions both to attract and repel. For those who understand themselves to be "insiders," the Johannine writings provide a remarkably strong sense of identity because of the clear distance they establish from "outsiders." Those same high identity markers can also serve to exacerbate a sense of alienation among readers less confident of being insiders.

Social dynamics do not, however, adequately account for the literary power of these writings. Their Greek style is simple. Yet every serious reader of these books knows how they compel attention through the complex web of symbols they construct. John's Jesus remains mysteriously elusive even as he discloses himself; the visions of Revelation are phantasmagoric and majestic. If a school was responsible for writing these books, it counted at least one or two poetic imaginations among its members.

A church divided: the letters

Two of the three letters (known as 2 and 3 John) are written by someone identified as the "Elder" and have the appearance of genuine letters; the third (1 John) has no epistolary elements and is probably a sermon or discourse. The reason all three compositions survived is probably due to the fact that they were sent at the same time to the same destination as part of a three-letter packet. They are literarily related and provide a window onto one moment in a divided Johannine Christianity.

Third John is a letter of commendation such as those written by community leaders to certify emissaries sent from one church to another. In this case, the Elder sends an emissary named Demetrius to a certain Gaius. The Elder praises Gaius for the hospitality shown the people he has sent out. Such welcome is a sign that he "walks in the truth" (3). Note how important such hospitality is for a sectarian movement, whose members are "accepting nothing from the pagans" (7). The Elder regards such hospitality as a form of participation in the work for the truth. He is therefore confident that Gaius will also accept the emissary Demetrius, who is recommended by everyone, and "even from the truth itself" (12).

The letter reveals an anxiety caused by internal divisions that complicate practices of mission and hospitality. The Elder complains of a certain Diotrephes, who "wants to hold first place" (9), spreads false rumors about the Elder, and refuses to receive the Elder's emissaries. Indeed, Diotrephes goes so far as to excommunicate those who do receive the Elder's delegates (10). There is clearly a struggle for power between the Elder and Diotrephes, each of whom claims authority over assemblies across a certain region and sends out delegates to secure that authority. In this struggle, hospitality and excommunication appear as weapons for the exercise of power.

The Elder declares that he has much to write to Gaius, but will not put pen to paper, hoping instead to communicate face to face (13, 14). Instead, he has "written something for the church" (9). It is this additional writing that Demetrius undoubtedly carries with him.

While 3 John is entirely personal—the subjects and verbs are singular rather than plural—2 John appears as something of a cover letter to a local assembly, undoubtedly the one in which Gaius exercises leadership. The designation "Elect Lady" in the greeting (2 John 1) symbolizes the church, whose members are "children." In contrast to 3 John, the subjects and verbs are plural: it is the congregation as such that is being addressed. This short missive provides the framework for the longer treatise that will be read to the gathered assembly, namely, 1 John.

Second John fills out the picture of conflict being experienced by these assemblies. It is not merely a matter of a power play among leaders. It involves a certain understanding of Christ. In typical sectarian fashion, this letter speaks of those who "have gone out into the world"—that is, left the assembly aligned with the Elder. The reason for the split is doctrinal: those who left "do not confess that Jesus Christ has come in the flesh" (2 John 7). And since they do not properly grasp Christ but have left, they are "the antichrist," and dangerous.

Remarkably, the Elder then recommends to this assembly that they do precisely what he has complained that Diotrephes was doing. They are not to receive into their households anyone teaching the false doctrine, for to welcome such a teacher means that one "shares in his evil works" (11).

Demetrius carried still a third composition with him as he traveled from the Elder to the assembly meeting in the household of Gaius. This is the "something for the church" mentioned in 3 John 9. It has come to be called "the first letter of John," but it was composed to be read aloud as a public address to the assembly. If Demetrius was making the rounds of local assemblies aligned with the Elder, he may well have had this as the circular message read in each church, together with the smaller notes to local communities and leaders.

First John reveals the sectarian struggle in this form of early Christianity. It speaks of those who "have gone out from us" (2:19) into the world that is darkness (1:11) and lies under the power of the evil one (5:19). They are false prophets (4:1) and the antichrist (2:18, 22; 4:3). There is poignancy in its declaration concerning those who had left: "They went out from us, but they were not really of our number; for if they had been, they would have remained with us" (2:19).

The cause of division is a disputed understanding of Christ. Unfortunately, the actual statements concerning what is professed and denied (2:22; 3:23; 4:2–3; 5:1) make it difficult to know precisely what aspect of Christ was at issue—most scholars think that Christ's full humanity was what was being denied by those who had "gone out."

Despite the pronounced "insider" perspective of 1 John, the composition is far more nuanced than much other sectarian literature. There is, for example, no attack on outsiders; instead, the author reminds insiders of their own failings (1:1—2:11). Such a turn to self-criticism within a sectarian writing is unexpected. John's statements alternate between the confidence of "we are" (in the light, in the truth, see 1:1–4) and the "we ought" of those chastened by failure. Likewise striking are three positive theological emphases. The author insists first on God's transcendence: No one has ever seen God (4:12); God is greater than the human heart (3:20). Such an insistence mitigates the tendency of remnant communities to claim perfect knowledge.

The author also reminds his readers that God is known above all in love—indeed, "God is love"—so that those "who are without love do not know God" (4:7). He speaks of the divine self-giving that is to be shared and expressed among humans: "Beloved, if God so loved us, we also must love one another" (4:11). Such love does not arise from human instinct, but is learned by the community from the love God showed in Jesus Christ (4:7–16).

Finally, the author declares that the love of God must be expressed through love of others (4:20–21) and that this commandment of love is fulfilled only when it is spelled out in concrete gestures of care for others: "If someone who has worldly goods sees a brother in need and refuses him compassion, how can the love of God remain in him?" (3:17)

Jesus reveals God: the Fourth Gospel

The most significant composition produced by Johannine Christianity is the Gospel according to John. It had an obvious and important role in shaping classical Christian doctrines concerning God and Christ, above all the doctrine of the incarnation: the teaching that in Jesus Christ, God was truly present in human history. This Gospel has always been the favorite of Christian mystics, who love its sense of mystery and the way in which its simple language invites intimacy while resisting complete access. Many ordinary Christians tend to think of John as communicating the fullest truth about Jesus. If asked, "What did Jesus do?" they would respond in terms of the Synoptic stories and sayings. But if they were asked, "Who is Jesus?" they would answer in terms of the Fourth Gospel.

The immediate impression given by this Gospel is how different it is from the Synoptic Gospels. The facts of Jesus' ministry are different. John has Jesus' ministry extend through three years rather than one. His activity centers in Judea instead of Galilee. He performs a prophetic gesture in the Temple at the start of his ministry, not at the end (Jn 2:13–21). His final meal with his disciples is not a Passover meal, and he does not interpret the bread and wine in terms of his death—instead, he washes his disciples' feet (13:1–11). His crucifixion occurs on a different date than in the Synoptics; it is explicitly correlated with the time when the lambs were slaughtered in preparation for the Passover feast (19:31). Although John provides an empty-tomb story, it is entirely unlike the one that appears in the Synoptics (20:1–10). The same is the case with the appearances of Jesus to his followers after his resurrection (20:11–29; 21:1–14).

The character of Jesus' ministry also appears different. The action of Jesus most highlighted by the Synoptics, namely the exorcism of those possessed by unclean spirits, is absent from John's account. The seven miracles Jesus does perform are called "signs." They include variant versions of healings in the other Gospels: John's blind man resembles none found in the Synoptics (9:1–7), and his healed paralytic appears in completely different circumstances (5:1–9).

Jesus also speaks differently in the John's Gospel. He tells none of the parables that so characterize the other Gospels—the few "figures" used by Jesus in the Fourth Gospel (10:6; 16:25–28) pale by comparison. John has no self-contained controversy stories pitting Jesus against his opponents and concluding with a sharply phrased aphorism or pronouncement. Controversies in John tend to extend themselves, and they turn into self-revelatory monologues (as in 3:12–21; 5:19–47; 6:26–65).

There are sufficient points of contact to make John recognizable as a Christian Gospel. John shares the same range of designations for Jesus: he is Messiah (1:41), Son of Man (1:51), Son of God (11:27), Prophet (6:14), King (1:49), and Savior (4:42). Some of Jesus' miracles are recognizably the same; above all the sequence of the multiplication of the loaves (6:1–15) and the walking on the water (6:16–21) is found both in John and the Synoptics.

Other events may be differently cast or placed, but are manifestly part of the same tradition, such as the entry into Jerusalem (12:12–19), the purification of the Temple (2:13–22), and the anointing at Bethany (12:1–10). Still other Synoptic stories happen "off stage" in John, such as the baptism of Jesus (1:29–34), or are found not in single stories but in more diffused references, such as the temptations (see 6:15), and Jesus' moment of decision before his arrest (12:27–29). Above all, John's passion account, though having its distinctive elements—such as the formal scene before Pilate (19:1–16) and Jesus' final words from the cross (19:26–30)—corresponds closely to the versions found in the Synoptic Gospels.

How can the relation of John to the other three Gospels best be stated? It is clear that there is no direct literary relationship to any of the other three, as there is among the Synoptics. Yet even when his reshaping is dramatic, John also clearly draws from the traditions shared by the other three. Some have thought of John as supplementary to the Synoptics in a material sense: he provides a larger ministry and reports things the Synoptics do not. But this view ignores his profound reshaping of everything. Others have thought of John as the "spiritual Gospel" that provides the heart of Jesus' identity rather than merely the physical events. But this ignores the "spiritual" dimensions of the first three Gospels as well as the very physical dimensions of John's account.

A better view of the relationship sees John as making explicit what is implicit in the Synoptic tradition. They implicitly portray Jesus as the revealer of God, but it is cast in terms of his knowing the moment of God's rule and his call to repent in response to his call. John states flatly from the beginning that Jesus reveals the Father (1:18). The Synoptic account of Jesus' multiplication of the loaves suggests his power over creation. John has Jesus identify himself as the bread of life that has come down from heaven (6:22–59). The Synoptics imply that the way humans respond to Jesus is the way they respond to God: "the one who receives you, receives me, and the one who receives me receives the one who sent me" (Lk 10:16). John explicitly makes the decision for or against Jesus the decision for or against God (12:44–50).

The Gospel is equally explicit about its own process of composition. The original ending of the Gospel declares that its treatment of Jesus is both selective and shaped for the purpose of reinforcing the faith of believers (20:30–31). Although it claims to derive from an eyewitness (see 19:35)—and its knowledge of first-century Palestine supports the origin of its traditions in that setting—the Gospel everywhere reveals a many-layered process of composition. The most obvious example is the addition of an epilogue (21:1–25), which uses a resurrection appearance of Jesus in Galilee to deal with the issues raised by the unanticipated death of the Beloved Disciple and the martyrdom of Peter.

John's narrative explicitly includes the perspective given by later experience. As Jesus speaks with the Jewish leader Nicodemus, the verbs suddenly shift in 3:11 from the singular to the plural, revealing the ongoing debates between Johannine believers and members of the synagogue. John reads the expulsion of believers from the synagogue back into the ministry of Jesus himself (9:22). And Jesus declares to his followers that the Holy Spirit that will be given to them after his glorification (=ascent to the Father) will lead them into a deeper understanding of what he had said and done (16:12–15).

The Gospel narrative candidly acknowledges the deeper insight given by the resurrection and the gift of the Spirit. Thus, when Jesus had cleansed the Temple and speaks of raising up the destroyed Temple in three days (2:19), the narrator observes in response to the Jews' incredulity, "But he was speaking of the temple of his body. Therefore, when he was raised from the dead, his disciples remembered what he had said, and they came to believe the Scripture and the word Jesus had spoken" (2:21–22).

The Fourth Gospel is stylistically simple, structurally straightforward, and symbolically subtle. Its Greek presents few linguistic challenges. Similarly, the structure of the work lacks complexity. The Gospel opens with a prologue (1:1–18) written in poetic strophes (with prose interjections in 1:6–8 and 1:15). The prologue introduces the reader to the Gospel's symbolism (light and darkness, life and death) as well as to the pattern of descent and ascent found throughout the narrative (Jesus is the one who comes from God and returns to God 1:18; see 13:1).

The prologue is followed by the account of Jesus' open ministry, usually called "The Book of Signs." It is dominated by the seven wonders ("signs") performed by Jesus. They reveal the divine presence (his "glory," 1:14; 2:11), stimulate controversy among his Jewish opponents, and lead to Jesus' self-revealing monologues. The classic example is Jesus' multiplication of the loaves for the multitude (6:1–15), which leads to his statement that he is the bread of life (6:35), and when this leads to controversy, his declaration that the bread he gives is his flesh for the life of the world (6:51).

The period of open ministry generates ever greater hostility among the leaders of the Jews and concludes with Jesus withdrawing from the public (12:36), declaring solemnly that the Jews' rejection of him was due to the fact that "they preferred human praise to the glory of God" (12:43).

The "Book of Glory" consists of two parts. In the first section (13:1—17:26), John places all of Jesus' explicit teaching to his disciples in the context of his last meal with them. He speaks directly to them of who he is and where he is going, of the unity that exists between the father and him (a unity they share), and of the hostility they will face from the world because they belong to him. He concludes with an extended prayer that they will be "consecrated in truth" (17:19).

The second section of the Book of Glory recounts the path by which Jesus returns to God and his place of "glory" (that is, God's presence), namely, his suffering, death, and resurrection (18:1–31). The composition as we now have it includes the epilogue (21:1–25) that predicts the destiny of Peter and the Beloved Disciple from whom this tradition derived.

In contrast to its open style and clear structure, the Gospel of John's symbolism is dense and evocative. Everything and everyone in this Gospel represents something else, points beyond itself to something larger. Sometimes the evangelist's touch is subtle. The careful reader notes that the prologue starts with the evocation of Genesis 1:1, "In the beginning," and that—for no obvious reason—the narrator then marks the passing of days (1:29, 35, 43), before deliberately observing that it was on "the third day" that Jesus turned water into wine at the Cana wedding feast (2:1). John insinuates that this act of "new creation" (itself bearing allusions to Christian baptism and eucharist), which "revealed his glory" (2:11), fulfills the seven days of the first creation, with "the third day" additionally bearing resonances of the day of resurrection.

John makes distinctive use of the traditional Jewish feasts within his narrative. At the most obvious level, the feasts of Passover (2:13; 6:4; 13:1), Booths (7:2—9:41), and Dedication of the Temple (10:22) serve as occasions for the gathering of people to witness Jesus' words and deeds. But John uses the symbolism attached to these feasts—as well as the Sabbath and the Jerusalem Temple itself—to help construct the portrait of Jesus.

The Jewish feasts serve as a primary means by which John can express Jesus' superiority to Torah. The theme is struck explicitly in the prologue: "The law was given through Moses, grace and truth came through Jesus Christ" (1:17). This statement explains the cryptic declaration immediately preceding it: "From his fullness (that is, of the Word made flesh) we have all received, grace in place of grace" (1:16). The Jewish Law given through Moses was, in short, a gift from God, but the fullness of that gift is found in Christ, who represents "fullness" and the "grace and truth" that are the very essence of the God of Israel (see Ex 34:6).

Above all, John uses the symbolism of the feast of Passover. In chapter 6, Jesus' multiplication of the loaves (6:1–15) is followed by a "passing over the sea" as Jesus walks on the sea (6:16–21), and when Jesus speaks of himself as the bread of life, John has him draw an explicit contrast between himself and the manna that was given to the ancient people through Moses: "Your ancestors ate manna in the desert and died; this is the bread that comes down from heaven so that one may eat it and not die. I am the living bread that came down from heaven; whoever eats this bread will live forever" (6:49–51). Similarly, John places Jesus' death at the moment when lambs were slaughtered in preparation for the Passover and uses a scriptural allusion that explicitly identifies Jesus as the "lamb of God" who is slain for the life of the world (19: 36; see 1:29).

All of John's symbolism centers in Christ. The series of "I am" statements made by Jesus range from straightforward metaphor—

light (8:12), bread (6:35), gate (10:7), shepherd (10:14), vine (15:1)—to claims of exclusive access to God ("I am the way and the truth and the life; no one comes to the father except through me," 14:6), and even to identity with God, as when Jesus declares simply, "I am" (6:20, evoking the divine disclosure to Moses in Ex 3:14). The import is plain in 8:56–59. While arguing with Jewish leaders about his identity, Jesus claims, "Abraham your father rejoiced to see my day; he saw it and was glad." His opponents understandably object that he is not yet fifty years old; how could he have seen Abraham? Jesus replies, "Amen, Amen, I say to you, before Abraham came to be, I am."

Jesus is a living symbol because he represents God (1:18). The symbolism of light coming into the darkness expresses the conviction of this Gospel that in Jesus, the claim of God on creation and the choice for or against God made by humans—a drama played out everywhere and at all times implicitly—is made explicit in the self-disclosure of God in Christ and the way in which humans accepted or rejected him (3:16–21).

Because Jesus is made to represent God within the narrative, John's Gospel inevitably lacks some of the realism found in the other Gospels. John insists on Jesus' humanity, but because he is made to speak for God, to be, indeed, the Word made flesh (1:14), his humanity is overshadowed by the intimations of the divine in his portrayal.

Indeed, all the characters in this Gospel are "representative," so that the narrative resembles a morality play. If Jesus represents God, then the disciples represent the believing world, and Pilate the skeptical world of politics. The downside of this literary technique is most apparent in John's portrayal of the Jews, who are made to represent, fatefully, the world that rejects God. The consequences of this blunt characterization have been evident in the powerful strain of anti-Semitism that has run through Christian history.

Heavens opened: Revelation

Some scholars doubt that the book of Revelation comes from the same Johannine circle that produced the letters and Gospel, so different is its style and, on the surface, its outlook. But it clearly shares with other Johannine writings a view of the world shaped by conflict, a view that in Revelation is given form by the use of the apocalyptic genre.

Readers who have not grasped the way apocalyptic works literarily have either been repulsed by the imagery of the book or misinterpreted it, often with sad results. Revelation has caused mischief among people who have taken it as a unique revelation from God about the future. Its powerful poetry has infiltrated a variety of private and public delusional systems. Read as a literal prediction of the end-time, this composition continues to hold a place of special importance for Christians who are called "Millenarians," so named because they anticipate a thousand-year earthly reign of the Messiah (Rev 20:4).

Here is a case where historically informed literary judgment is critical to responsible interpretation. The word "revelation" is in Greek "apocalypse," a term that denotes the disclosure of realities previously hidden. Revelation is one of the two classic representatives of apocalyptic literature in the Bible, and it is best understood when the characteristics of that genre are appreciated. The book of Daniel is the first full-fledged expression of this Jewish literary form. Composed around 167 BCE, when the Hellenistic king Antiochus IV was oppressing Jews in Palestine, it displays all the features of the literary genre and view of history known as apocalyptic.

Apocalyptic is a form of resistance literature for those who experience themselves as marginalized or oppressed. In the period between 167 BCE and 200 CE, it was a favorite mode of composition for Jews who resisted Roman rule and Hellenistic culture. Written in the name of a hero of the past (Adam or Enoch or Daniel), it is fictive prophecy, interpreting the events of the present as though foreseen by an ancient figure. Apocalyptic features experiences of heavenly ascent or dreams that provide visions of the present (in heaven) and future (on earth). The seer expresses such visions in highly coded language, employing numbers, fabulous personified beasts, and cosmic phenomena as symbols whose meaning is available only to insiders.

Despite its complex imagery, the apocalyptic understanding of history is simple: it has a goal that is in God's hands. Although evidence may seem to suggest otherwise, with oppression triumphant, God is actually in charge and will bring about a dramatic change. The turn from this world to "the world to come" is a turn from the oppression of the righteous to the rule of the righteous. It is brought about by divine agency, a "Son of Man" or a "Messiah," who will deliver the people and give them dominion over their human enemies. Equally straightforward is the religious message of apocalyptic. It encourages the oppressed to remain loyal to God, in the conviction that they will see their reward.

The book of Revelation clearly fits within the apocalyptic framework. There is the heavenly ascent of the Seer who gazes on the heavenly court and sees what will happen below. The visions involve symbolic numbers (4s and 7s and 12s), personified beasts (notably the one named 666 in Rev 13:11–18), and cosmic catastrophes. The vision of history is one of conflict between God and the "dragon, that ancient serpent, who is the Devil and Satan" (20:2), played out in the human arena as the oppression of the saints by the evil empire, leading to God's final triumph on earth (20:4—22:7). The lesson for readers is classic: "Here is a call for the endurance and faith of the saints" (13:10).

In other ways, Revelation breaks the apocalyptic mold. The work is not pseudonymously ascribed to a figure of the past but to a contemporary, "John your brother" on the island of Patmos (1:9).

Above all, the symbolism of apocalyptic is re-catalyzed by the experience of the crucified and raised Messiah Jesus. The "one like a Son of Man" who appears to the Seer in the opening scene is Jesus: "I am the first and the last, and the living one. I was dead, and see, I am alive forever" (1:17). When the Seer ascends into the divine throne room in heaven, the one standing on the right

9. Matthias Scheits, *Bowls, the Dragon, the Woman on the Beast, and the Fall of Babylon*: *Revelation* depicts the battle between the saints and the evil powers of the Roman Empire.

hand of the throne is the lamb who was slain, who is praised by the living creatures and elders, "Worthy is the lamb that was slain to receive power and riches and wisdom and strength, and honor and glory and blessing" (5:11–12).

In contrast to the understanding of history that sees the present in terms of defeat and victory as solely a hope for the future, Revelation states that God's fundamental victory over evil and death has already been won. The first sign of this victory is the death and resurrection of Jesus, who now xercises divine dominion. The victory is not his alone: the Seer perceives as well the countless witnesses to Jesus who were put to death ("washed their robes and made them white in the blood of the lamb") and were now "before the throne of God and worship him day and night within his temple" (7:13–17).

The climax of history has already happened; the continuing struggle on earth is, strictly speaking, denouement. Although the final vision sees the New Jerusalem coming down from heaven from God, and God dwelling among humans, as a future event (21:1–8), the very first vision already shows the resurrected Jesus present among the "seven lampstands" that are the seven churches in Asia Minor (1:12–20). Contrary to superficial impressions, then, Revelation is profoundly optimistic.

A distinctive feature of Revelation is the inclusion of seven letters sent from the risen Jesus to the churches in Ephesus (2:1), Smyrna (2:8), Thyatira (2:18), Sardis (3:1), Philadelphia (3:7), and Laodicea (3:14). Here we find not visions of the future or the heavenly realm, but insight into the circumstances of specific assemblies in the major cities of a Roman province. The letters speak of failures and successes within the communities, measured by loyalty and apostasy, integrity and corruption. They show in what sense Revelation can legitimately be considered a prophetic book, not because it predicts the future, but because it addresses humans from the perspective of God's vision for the world.

The same prophetic outlook applies equally to the visions that begin in 4:1 and run to the end of the book. In them, the conflict is not with corruption and apostasy within specific assemblies but is a cosmic struggle between God and Satan (12:9). This cosmic battle also involves human agents. Representing the forces of evil is the empire (clearly identified in 17:1—18:24 as Rome), and representing God are those followers of Christ who have not yet faced martyrdom, yet are nevertheless called to bear witness. The meaning of the visions is not found in a point-by-point prediction of the future, but in an imaginative expression of the cosmic stakes in the human struggle for truth and integrity.

Revelation does not summon Christians to do violence against the forces of evil but rather to resist them by refusing to acknowledge their authority. Christians do not recognize the emperor as supreme. For them there is but one "Lord of lords and King of kings," and "those with him are called, chosen, and faithful" (17:14). Strengthened by the expression of God's victory imagined by the visions, they can witness by their lives to the one who bore witness to the death, by continuing his resistance to the powers of evil.

They do this by refusing to regard as ultimate the pretend-powers of human arrogance, and by "worshiping God" alone. It is fitting that Revelation concludes with the vision of God's people engaged in worship within the New Jerusalem: "The throne of God and of the Lamb will be in it, and his servants will worship him . . . the Lord their God will be their light, and they will reign for ever and ever" (22:3–5).

The powerful imagery of Revelation has done damage when it was literalized and made an escape from reality. But for many Christians throughout the centuries, as in the American civil rights struggle, the sense of participating in a larger world opened up by Revelation's opening of the heavens has provided encouragement for a resistance to evil that is firmly grounded in reality.

The Johannine literature as a whole continues to draw readers less because it is otherworldly than because it so clearly emerges from real-life contexts of conflict; it continues to fascinate readers because of the way it refuses to be simply defined by its origin in conflict, but uses the power of imagination to transcend sectarian splits through love (the letters), to overcome division through unity (the Gospel), and to resist evil through true worship (Revelation).

Chapter 10
Becoming the New Testament

The earliest Christian writings were not composed as sacred Scripture. They were incidental if not accidental compositions, written for the moment rather than the ages. They emerge from diverse circumstances in communities across the Mediterranean in the second half of the first century, and they reflect that diversity in their literary forms and religious perspectives. These writings became the New Testament—an extended appendix to the Jewish Scripture now designated as Old Testament—through a process of canonization that began almost immediately but lasted more than a hundred years, and was closely tied to the process of Christian self-definition.

The many separate assemblies became a unified "Christianity" or "church" also through shared convictions and practices, as well as through sharing possessions and cultivating personal networks. Nevertheless, the canonization of certain books as Scripture was a key element in Christianity's emergence in the late second century as a coherent and "catholic" (in the sense of universal) religion that could compete for adherents on equal terms with both Paganism and Judaism.

The process of canonization

The first stages were natural and organic, involving a dialectical relationship between texts and reading communities. Only at the last stage of ratification did canonization become an organization-wide formal decision.

The very composition of the New Testament writings involved the Jewish Scriptures in Greek translation as well as community traditions. Paul, for example, uses Scripture vigorously in his argument concerning Jews and Gentiles in Romans 9—11. Paul likewise uses traditions already in place within the movement he joined: rituals such as baptism and the Lord's Supper, for example; sayings of Jesus; and creedal formulations. Similarly, the Gospels construct their narratives about Jesus on the basis of traditions that were transmitted orally within communities, and they also deploy diverse aspects of the Jewish Scriptures in their portrayal of Jesus and the disciples.

The various New Testament compositions, in turn, were meant to be used within the assembly. Letters were read aloud by the delegates who delivered them. Gospel narratives were read aloud in the worship gathering. Such use identified these compositions as public documents and sped their identification as Christian "Scripture," since they joined the Jewish Scriptures in such public performance within the worship assembly.

The basic step toward canonization was the exchange of writings among Christian communities. As Colossians 4:16 suggests, such exchange had already taken place in Paul's ministry. Two sets of letters (1, 2, 3 John and Colossians, Ephesians, Philemon) suggest the practice of sending letters to several communities at once, accelerating the process of exchange. This stage is important because it marks the transition from the particular to the general, from the local to the universal: what Paul said in the past to the Corinthians is pertinent to a later generation in another place.

In the early second century, communities had gathered small collections of writings through such exchange. Clement of Rome writes to the Corinthians around 95 CE, making reference to

10. POxy. 1080, a fourth-century manuscript containing
Rev 3:19—4:3, with the last verses describing the Seer's ascent
to heaven.

sayings of Jesus as well as to 1 Corinthians, Hebrews, and James.
The early second-century letters of Ignatius and Polycarp likewise
reveal knowledge of the Gospels of Matthew and John, and
several of Paul's letters. The New Testament Second Letter of
Peter—probably written in the early second century—refers to
"all the letters of Paul," as though they existed in a collection, and

alludes to a tradition of interpretation of those letters "as with all the Scripture" (2 Pet 3:16).

To this point, though, such community collections were informal, and references to the New Testament writings are not by explicit citation so much as by allusion. There is no need for an official list of writings because the accepted compositions have not yet been challenged by addition or subtraction.

The critical stage for canonization and Christian self-definition came in the mid-second century. Two challenges arose to the received compositions that are the earliest attested in the Christian movement. Both challenges involved books and ideologies. A move to reduce the collection came from Marcion, who as a function of his intensely dualistic worldview rejected the God of the Old Testament as the fashioner of evil matter and thought that only Paul properly understood Jesus as the liberator of the spirit from the flesh. Marcion therefore argued that only ten of Paul's letters (absent the Pastorals) and Luke's Gospel made up a theologically consistent canon, and he rejected the rest of the received compositions as "Judaizing," that is, reverting to the Jewish God.

The other challenge came from forces of expansion, represented above all by the prolific production of revelatory compositions by powerful teachers known to history as Gnostics. Once more, the dominant ideology reflected by diverse literary forms was profoundly dualistic, advancing a version of Christianity that privileged the soul of the individual—and its liberation from the flesh—more than the corporate body of the assembly. Together, these literary and ideological challenges forced the selection of books to be regarded as normative for the community.

We know of these compositions partly through the rebuttals of them offered by late second-century "orthodox" teachers such as

Irenaeus of Lyons and Tertullian of Carthage, and partly through the recovery of the long-buried library of Coptic texts. Both make clear the seriousness of the challenge.

In his *Against Heresies*, Irenaeus of Lyons (ca. 180) shaped the classic response to these challenges that defined orthodox Christianity in terms of a public, institutional, and inclusive religion. In his rebuttal of various Gnostic ideologies, Irenaeus constructed a remarkably sturdy strategy for ecclesial self-definition. He countered the claim of secret teachings by appeal to the "Rule of Faith" (or creed), a public expression of belief that summarized the Christian myth and provided a guide to the reading of its compositions.

Irenaeus answered the claim to secret revelatory books by appeal to the books received from the apostles—a canon of Scripture embracing the Old Testament, all the letters of Paul, four (and only four) Gospels, and other "catholic" writings. Finally, he responded to the Gnostic claim of secret teachers by appealing to the public "apostolic succession" of bishops appointed by the apostles—all of whom, he claimed, professed these beliefs and read only these books. From the time of Irenaeus, challenges to Christian belief or practice were answered by the meeting of bishops in council, who, on the basis of the canon of Scripture, expanded or defended the creed.

The position taken by Irenaeus and Tertullian was accepted by a variety of other bishops and teachers, including such adventuresome Alexandrian thinkers as Clement and Origen. By the late fourth century, both individual bishops, such as Athanasius (in his Paschal Letter of 364), and councils, such as that in Carthage (in 397), ratified the stance taken by the defenders of the mainstream tradition.

Although the question of the canon was posed in a minor way during the Protestant Reformation, the classic collection called the New Testament remained stable since the late second century. After the discovery of the Gnostic library at Nag Hammadi in 1945, and the development of ideological criticism within scholarship (above all feminism), the issue of canon was again joined in certain quarters, but there is little likelihood that the great majority of Christian traditions will either expand or contract the collection that has shaped Christian life and thought for two thousand years.

Criteria for canonization

This historical sketch is broad but substantially accurate. Despite popular opinions to the contrary, the compositions now included in the New Testament genuinely are the earliest evidences for Christianity. Even scholars who claim more primitive elements in some Gnostic compositions (above all the Coptic Gospel of Thomas) acknowledge that the Gospel of Thomas itself is at best a mid-second-century production.

Nevertheless, many other compositions were written in the late and early second century, so that the question of the criteria employed in canonization is legitimate, especially since the evidence also suggests that some compositions, such as "The Shepherd of Hermas," enjoyed strong local authority.

The criterion of divine inspiration—perhaps surprisingly to some present-day readers—is rarely if ever invoked. The New Testament compositions were regarded as inspired, but inspiration did not mark them as distinctive. Early Christianity saw many forms of inspired utterance and visionary revelations—not excluding the Gnostic compositions. The New Testament writings, furthermore, do not claim divine inspiration for themselves, only for the Jewish Scriptures (2 Tim 3:16).

More often, the criterion of apostolicity is applied. In one way or another, the New Testament compositions are connected to apostles. This criterion also is scarcely fail-proof: a number of the Gnostic compositions claim to come from apostles, after all, and it is a struggle to connect some New Testament compositions to an apostle; among the evangelists, for example, Mark is claimed to be a translator of Peter, Luke a companion of Paul.

The claim of apostolicity is at heart a statement of historical priority: the traditional collection precedes the compositions that were composed in the second century and derive from the earliest Christian witnesses. Thus the argument is made that the visible successors of the apostles, the bishops, read these books and professed these beliefs and none other.

The most important criterion for canonization was probably an instinct, or "sense of the church," a perception of fit between the community and this particular set of writings that extended through time: these were the compositions that had shaped Christians from the beginning; these are the compositions that reflect the canonizers' sense of what it means to be church, that is, a public and institutional assembly of believers committed to the body, the world, and history; and these will be the writings that can transmit that vision of the church to the future.

Implications of canonization

Canonization made a collection of twenty-seven disparate writings from the first century into the New Testament and thereby part of the Christian Scripture. But canon is more than a historical fact. It continues to form a certain kind of Christianity whenever it is affirmed as one of the constitutive elements of this religion. Such affirmation is a religious decision by present-day communities rather than a historical conclusion.

The decision has a number of implications. The most important is that these ancient compositions retain their significance for every Christian in every age and circumstance. Canonization is a statement of relevance. Indeed, it defines Scripture as prophetic, as speaking for God to humans in every age. The historical meaning of the text is not, in this perspective, the only or even the most important meaning: the letters of Paul and James, as well as the Gospels, continue to speak to present-day readers much as they did to their first readers.

Two paradoxical consequences of canonization are of particular importance. The first is that by affirming the Jewish Scriptures as its "Old Testament" and continuing to read them as its own Scripture, Christians established an inevitable and tension-filled conversation with Jews through the ages, who continue to read Torah from their own perspective. For the most part, Christians have sought to dictate the terms of the conversation from a position of presumed superiority and have still to learn how to conduct that conversation on even terms with Jews.

The second important paradox is that the act of canonization, which sought to establish unity, actually institutionalized diversity. While it is perfectly true that the twenty-seven writings of the New Testament have a family resemblance not shared by apocryphal writings, a family resemblance that serves to form a certain kind of Christianity among those who read them, it is equally true that they still retain all the diversity of genre, perspective, and even opinion that they had from the beginning. Because of this irreducible diversity, Christians through the ages have managed to produce a bewildering variety of institutional structures, theologies, rituals, and even moralities, all while sincerely claiming to take the New Testament with utmost seriousness.

Chapter 11
The pertinence of the New Testament

Imagine that the plays of William Shakespeare were performed every week in theaters dedicated exclusively to the Bard throughout the world—and had been continuously since he wrote them—and that they had been translated into every human language and virtually every dialect. Imagine that they sold at a rate greater than any other book ever published, and that they were the subject of analysis in thousands of scholarly works each year and in many more thousand popular books and articles.

Imagine that Shakespeare was the center of passionate classroom debate in hundreds of schools throughout the world founded precisely on the basis of his plays. Imagine that his plays were not only the most quoted of all human writings, but also the most intensely studied by hundreds of millions of people around the globe as the indispensable guide to their lives.

If we can imagine such things, then it would appear to be easy to make the case that the plays of William Shakespeare were pertinent to the present day. Such is also the case with the New Testament. Everything suggested hypothetically about Shakespeare's plays is actually the case with the New Testament: its use in worship weekly and even daily throughout the world, its universal translation, its sales, study, and devoted readership. That hundreds of millions of present-day humans claim to take the New Testament seriously cannot seriously be challenged.

Going back to the analogy, some may offer three objections to the pervasive presence and influence of Shakespeare's plays. It is a mistake for humans to devote so much attention to Elizabethan dramaturgy. At best it is a distraction from serious endeavors; at worst it cultivates an unhealthy aestheticism.

Moreover, most enactments of Shakespeare are poorly done; the plays are misinterpreted, the performances inept; the great dramatist is betrayed by those who most claim to love him.

Finally, Shakespeare is full of attitudes that are bad for people: he is misogynistic, anti-Semitic, bellicose, and chauvinistic, and he displays any number of other qualities that fall below present-day social values.

The very same objections can and have been made to the influence of the New Testament. Those who despise religion generally and Christianity in particular find the persistent pertinence of the New Testament in contemporary life a deep if puzzling irritant. How can so many people be duped by such ancient superstition? Despite the aggressive resistance to Christianity among many contemporary intellectuals, however, Christianity refuses to die. Indeed, it grows and prospers in many regions of the world.

A second objection is similar to the one that says Shakespeare is performed badly or with little understanding. Who will argue with the statement that the vast majority of those who read the New Testament do so with less than adequate understanding, or even that the vast majority of them live in a manner that is in one respect or another inconsistent with it? Lack of understanding and even failures in performance, however, do not detract from the fact that the writings of the New Testament continue to stand as the measure of human life for most of those who read it. Indeed, just as bad performances of Shakespeare at least keep Shakespeare in circulation and available to more intelligent and better performances and, miraculously, do not actually harm the texts themselves beyond repair, so do the inadequate lives of Christians at least keep the New Testament compositions alive and available for more responsible readings and more faithful lives.

The final objection, that the pertinence of the New Testament is the more unfortunate because its influence is so toxic, is widespread among a variety of critics today. They point out the many ways in which the New Testament is thought to have created, or at least supported, inhumane and suppressive tendencies among Christians. They complain that the New Testament took the joy out of sex. They note, accurately enough, that Christian anti-Semitism traditionally drew its venom from the vitriol directed toward Jews by early Christians. They observe how intolerance toward heretics in New Testament compositions lent credibility to the suppression of diversity in faith communities. They charge the New Testament writers, above all Paul, with sexist attitudes that led to women's voices being silenced for centuries.

All such charges have an element, even a considerable element, of truth. And a further charge might be added, namely, that by its consistent manner of demonizing Gentile religion, the New Testament supported centuries of Christian hostility toward other world religions.

It is insufficient to answer such charges by observing that for some of them, at least, the New Testament contains positive as well as negative elements. It is not that Paul denigrates sex, but that he makes it so interpersonally important, that makes his stance problematic for those wanting it only to be casual. John does declare that salvation comes from the Jews, for example, and Paul does pray that all Israel will be saved. The Paul who tells women to be silent in the assembly was, in fact, the most liberated of all ancient writers when it came to women's public participation in activities outside the household.

Such responses are insufficient because, in fact, the toxic elements are nevertheless there, and they can be read and put into action by those whose dispositions already incline them toward narrowness, hostility, and venom. Not only history but the headlines show this to be so.

The appropriate response to the critics is much the same as it would be for Shakespeare's plays. Yes, they are performed poorly and without understanding; yes, they contain potentially harmful elements. But look at what escapes all that mangling by readers and actors! Look at all the beauty, grandeur, profundity, wisdom, humor, sheer humanity that remains when all the objections have been made. Look at all the gorgeous verse, the immortal lines that still stun the unwary reader. Look at the way in which his plays elevate the spirits and enhance the humanity of those who parse and perform them.

The New Testament, for all its manifold and manifest faults, similarly—indeed, superlatively—retains the capacity to stir human hearts, transform human freedom, stimulate human service to humanity. If the New Testament has been the tool of tyranny in the hands of the wicked, so has it also been the great resource of those saints whose energies were bent to the liberation of others.

Jesus' Sermon on the Mount (Matt 5—7), Paul's Hymn of Love (1 Cor 13), the depiction of the first believers sharing all their possessions (Acts 4:32–37), Jesus' call to abandon everything and give everything away for the sake of the kingdom and for the sake of the world's poor (Lk 12:22–34; 14:26–33)—these words bear no taint of evil, no stain of selfishness, and these are the words that the saints, through history and still today, turn to in support of their generous and world-enhancing lives.

The canonical arrangement of the New Testament

The Gospel of Matthew

The Gospel of Mark

The Gospel of Luke

The Gospel of John

The Acts of the Apostles

The Letter of Paul to the Romans

The First Letter of Paul to the Corinthians

The Second Letter of Paul to the Corinthians

The Letter of Paul to the Galatians

The Letter of Paul to the Ephesians

The Letter of Paul to the Philippians

The Letter of Paul to the Colossians

The First Letter of Paul to the Thessalonians

Chronology

BCE (Before the Common Era)

323	Death of Alexander the Great
168	Roman Domination of Mediterranean War of Maccabees against Antiochus IV
167	Book of Daniel
63	Conquest of Palestine by Pompey
30	Augustus becomes Emperor
6	Judaea annexed as Province by Rome
4	Birth of Jesus (probable)

CE (The Common Era)

28	Ministry of John the Baptist
30	Crucifixion of Jesus (probable)
34/37	Conversion of Paul (probable)
49–64	Ministry and Letters of Paul Other Epistles (James, Hebrews) Oral tradition in assemblies
64	Nero burns Rome, blames Christians
66	Jewish War against Rome
68	Death of Paul and Peter (probable)

70	Destruction of Temple by Romans
	Gospel of Mark (probable)
85	Birkat ha Minim
	Gospel of Matthew
	Luke-Acts
90	Gospel of John
95	First Clement
96	Persecution under Domitian
	Revelation
107	Martyrdom of Ignatius of Antioch
122–135	Final Jewish Revolts against Rome
135	Destruction of Jerusalem by Romans
135/6	Gnostic Valentinus in Rome
155	Martyrdom of Polycarp
160	Death of (heretic) Marcion
165	Martyrdom of Justin
156/70	Ministry of Montanus (approximate)
200	Death of Irenaeus
313	Edict of Milan (Constantine)
325	Council of Nicaea
367	Athanasius' Paschal Letter
397	Council of Carthage

Further reading

Annotated Bibles

Attridge, Harold W., ed. *The HarperCollins Study Bible*. Rev. ed. San Francisco: HarperSanFrancisco, 2006.

Coogan, Michael D., ed. *The New Oxford Annotated Bible with the Apocrypha*. 3rd augmented ed., New York: Oxford University Press, 2004.

Senior, Donald, and John J. Collins, eds. *The Catholic Study Bible*. 2nd ed. New York: Oxford University Press, 2006.

Reference

Achtemeier, Paul J., ed. *The HarperCollins Bible Dictionary*. San Francisco: HarperSanFrancisco, 1996.

Freedman, David Noel, ed. *The Anchor Bible Dictionary*. New York: Doubleday, 1992.

Hayes, John H., ed. *Dictionary of Biblical Interpretation*. Nashville: Abingdon, 1999.

Mays, James L., ed. *The HarperCollins Bible Commentary*. San Francisco: HarperSanFrancisco, 2000.

Newsom, Carol A., and Sharon H. Ringe, eds. *Women's Bible Commentary*. Expanded ed. Louisville, KY: Westminster John Knox Press, 1998.

Introductions

Brown, Raymond E. *An Introduction to the New Testament*. New York: Doubleday, 1997.

Holladay, Carl R. *A Critical Introduction to the New Testament: Interpreting the Message and Meaning of Jesus Christ*. Nashville: Abingdon, 2005.

Johnson, Luke T. *The Writings of the New Testament: An Interpretation*. 2nd rev. ed., with the assistance of T. C. Penner. Minneapolis: Fortress Press, 1999.

Canon

MacDonald, Lee M. *The Formation of the Christian Biblical Canon*. Rev. ed. Peabody, MA: Hendrickson Publishers, 1995.

Gospels

Brown, Raymond E. *The Gospel According to John*. 2 vols. Anchor Bible; Garden City, NY: Doubleday, 1966, 1970.

Overman, J. Andrew. *Church and Community in Crisis: The Gospel According to Matthew*. Valley Forge, PA: Trinity International Press, 1996.

Robbins, Vernon K. *Jesus the Teacher: a Socio-Rhetorical Interpretation of Mark*. Philadelphia: Fortress Press, 1984.

Tannehill, Robert C. *The Narrative Unity of Luke-Acts: A Literary Interpretation*. 2 vols. Philadelphia: Fortress Press, 1986, 1990.

Paul

Johnson, Luke T. *Reading Romans: A Literary and Theological Commentary*. New York: Crossroad, 1996.

Malherbe, Abraham J. *Paul and the Popular Philosophers*. Minneapolis: Fortress Press, 1989.

Meeks, Wayne A., and John T. Fitzgerald, eds. *The Writings of St. Paul: Annotated Texts, Reception and Criticism*. 2nd ed. New York: W. W. Norton, 2007.

Mitchell, Margaret M. *Paul and the Rhetoric of Reconciliation: An Exegetical Investigation of the Language and Composition of 1 Corinthians*. Louisville, KY: Westminster John Knox Press, 1991.

Segal, Alan F. *Paul the Convert: The Apostolate and Apostasy of Saul the Pharisee*. New Haven, CT: Yale University Press, 1990.

Other Writings

Aune, D. E. *Revelation*. 3 vols. Word Biblical Commentary; Dallas, TX: Word Books, 1997–98.

DeSilva, David A. *Perseverence in Gratitude: A Socio-Rhetorical Commentary on the Epistle "to the Hebrews."* Grand Rapids, MI: Eerdmans, 2000.

Johnson, Luke T. *Brother of Jesus, Friend of God: Studies in the Letter of James*. Grand Rapids, MI: Eerdmans, 2004.

Further reading

Index

Index

R

Index of biblical passages